American Painter in Paris:

A LIFE OF MARY CASSATT

"Portrait of the Artist." Mary Cassatt's self portrait, 1878

American Painter in Paris

A LIFE OF MARY CASSATT

by Ellen Wilson

An Ariel Book
FARRAR, STRAUS & GIROUX
New York

For my husband, William E. Wilson

ACKNOWLEDGMENTS

This book could never have been written without the help of many kind people—friends and strangers who became friends—far too many to be thanked individually here. However, I want to express my special gratitude to the relatives of Mary Cassatt who gave me invaluable assistance: Mrs. John B. Thayer, formerly Lois Cassatt, the painter's grandniece, who received me in her home and, with trusting generosity, lent me many personal letters written from France by Mary Cassatt to members of her family in the United States; Mrs. Horace Binney Hare, formerly Ellen Mary Cassatt, the painter's niece, who helped by writing an enlightening letter about the character and personality of her artist-aunt; and Mr. Alexander J. Cassatt, a grandnephew, who shared in correspondence personal reminiscences of his happy childhood visits to his aunt's château.

There are others, like the present Mrs. Gardner Cassatt and Mrs. Percy C. Madeira, Jr., who have been prompt and gracious in answering queries. Mrs. Madeira not only verified anecdotes about her famous aunt but has been more than generous in offering photographs for this book. Mrs. Eric de Spoelberch, too, has been warmly responsive.

vii

Mrs. Adelyn D. Breeskin, Curator of Contemporary Art, National Collection of Fine Arts, Smithsonian Institution, is justly acclaimed as the foremost Cassatt expert of today. She has been indefatigable in answering questions, in both conversations and correspondence, and was a continuing source of wise counsel. Her two *Catalogues Raisonnés* of Mary Cassatt's work offer the richest possible mine for the serious student of the artist's career.

Professors Theodore Bowie and John Jacobus of the Fine Arts Department of Indiana University have been helpful, and directors of many leading museums in this country and in France have aided in collecting illustrative materials. Their individual contributions and permissions are acknowledged elsewhere, but the name of Mr. E. John Bullard should have special mention here. As assistant director of the National Gallery of Art and co-ordinator for the largest Cassatt show ever presented (National Gallery of Art, September 27–November 8, 1970), he was extraordinarily helpful in obtaining many of the photographs in this book.

Wilma Sands in the Office of the Curator in The White House was so responsive in lending me photographic materials that through her it was proved again that the White House belongs to all Americans.

Louise Wallman, former registrar and archivist of the Pennsylvania Academy of the Fine Arts, extended invaluable aid in checking records of Mary Cassatt's early student days.

Through their hospitality, numerous friends have enhanced my pleasure in my research in art centers near their homes. Among them are: Dr. and Mrs. Paul A. Bishop of Philadelphia; Mr. and Mrs. John Bemis of Cleveland; Mr. and Mrs. Richard M. Cameron, Concord, Mass.; Mrs. Margaret Smyser Crane, New York City; Mr. and Mrs. A. D. Emmart, Baltimore; Mr. and Mrs. Keith Masters and Mr. and Mrs. Arthur Tebbutt, Chicago; Miss Jean Richmond, Wakefield, R.I.; and Mr. and Mrs. Douglas C. Wilson, Washington, D.C.

In Europe, people were equally cordial. Mme Simone Cammas, Conservateur of the Musée Départmental de l'Oise, and her assistant, Mlle Monique Quesnot, not only opened their files to me but escorted me to Mary Cassatt's Château de Beaufresne. There we had a happy day's visit in the company of M. and Mme Mathière, directors of the château, now a school and home for friendless boys.

Mlle Eléanore Dartey of Aix-en-Provence translated for this book the

viii

sonnet that Degas wrote to Miss Cassatt and her parrot. Mrs. Isabella Musa, native of Parma, translated from Italian critical descriptions of Correggio's works. Through good friends, Professor and Mrs. G. Haydn Huntley of Northwestern University and Ventimiglia, I was introduced to M. Sella of l'Hôtel du Cap d'Antibes, who, as knowledgeable historian of Antibes, was able to find for me the villa occupied by Mary Cassatt. Another friend, Mlle Odette Bornand of Mougins, acted as a helpful guide on this and other expeditions in France.

Affectionate heartfelt thanks are due M. Yvon Bizardel, Directeur Honoraire des Beaux-Arts de Paris. Not only did he provide letters of introduction to officials in the Louvre and the Petit Palais and share his vast knowledge of the art world of Paris, but he gave me the benefit of his own long study of and interest in Mary Cassatt. It was he who played an important role in organizing "L'Hommage à Mary Cassatt" at the Château de Beaufresne and the Musée at Beauvais in 1965. M. Bizardel welcomed me and made me feel at home in France.

A printed source of material of extraordinary value has been Mrs. Louisine W. Havemeyer's remarkable *Sixteen to Sixty: Memoirs of a Collector,* privately printed for her family by the Metropolitan Museum of New York. A close friend of Mary Cassatt, who advised her and her husband, Henry O. Havemeyer, in their art-collecting days, Mrs. Havemeyer had a uniquely perceptive view of the artist and her circle of Impressionist contemporaries.

Two authors of recent scholarly biographical studies of Mary Cassatt should also be given special mention as offering rich sources of material. Frederick A. Sweet, formerly of the Art Institute of Chicago, has given Cassatt devotées a lode star to follow in his volume, *Miss Mary Cassatt, Impressionist from Pennsylvania.* Julia M. H. Carson, too, has offered some fresh leads in her book, *Mary Cassatt.*

Most of all my gratitude goes to my husband, William E. Wilson, a writer, who has with understanding and good humor suffered with me through the growing pains of this book. He acted as interpreter and translator when the language became too difficult for me in France. He made my search for the scenes of Mary Cassatt's life a joyous one by accompanying me from Paris throughout most of France and back again to Paris, that city of delight that Mary Cassatt adopted as her own.

FOREWORD

Mary Cassatt, our foremost woman painter, has been the
subject of many scholarly and critical works. This book
makes no attempt to join that imposing company. It is,
rather, an account of her contradictory life and career and
her charming personality.

In the nineteenth century, a time when no proper young
lady in America could consider making art a professional
career, this proper young lady did. Why did she do it? How
did she do it? What did she gain? What did she lose? These
are some of the questions that this book tries to answer.

The answers are based on much reading and research
and much pondering. They are based on letters that Mary
Cassatt and her family wrote, on reminiscences of the
nieces and nephews who visited her and who as children

posed for her, and on the writings of contemporaries who were her friends: Degas, Renoir, Berthe Morisot and others.

From these and many other sources there emerges a portrait of Mary Cassatt, a young woman who refused to accept the current American attitude that the artist's world was a man's world. With courage she became a rebel; with talent and determination she became an artist; with grace she remained a lady. And always, as she said to her French biographer, she was "American . . . clearly and frankly American."

American Painter in Paris:

A LIFE OF MARY CASSATT

CHAPTER I

When Mary Cassatt woke up early on the 22nd of May in 1860, she remembered at once that this was to be a special day in her life. It was her sixteenth birthday, a day she had looked forward to with both eagerness and dread. Months ago she had decided that as soon as she was sixteen she must get up her courage to tell her family that she was determined to become an artist, a real artist. She could no longer be content with just dabbling at painting here in her own room.

Mary looked around her, remembering how happy she had been two years before when the Cassatts moved into the high brick house on Central Square in Philadelphia and she chose this third-floor bedroom just under the maids' quarters because it had a good north light. Her first studio!

It had been a wonderful workroom. But more and more Mary began to realize that she had gone as far as she could, painting by herself. She needed professional criticism and help; she would have to go away where she could work seriously and be taken seriously. It wouldn't be easy. It would take all her courage to tell her parents that she was resolved to make painting a career.

Most of all, Mary dreaded facing her dignified father. Although he was usually kind and indulgent, there were certain things that his daughters were expected to do, others that they just did not do. "Puttering with paints," as he put it, was all right as long as Mary kept her rather remarkable amateur talent at home.

"An amateur," Mary thought indignantly. "That is what I am and what I'll always be if I don't rebel now."

On the easel in her room was an almost finished canvas, a self-portrait. The portrait lacked technical skill, but it did look something like her. Here were her wide-apart gray eyes, looking straight ahead, intent and serious. The end of her rather large nose was slightly upturned. Her pointed chin was thrust forward. Mary had not flattered herself in the least. All the separate features were definitely here, but the total effect was wrong. There was no depth, no character in it; none of her lively intelligence was there.

"In some ways it's a good likeness," Mary thought as she studied it, "but it's a poor painting. The worst of it is, I don't know what to do to make it right."

Mary looked across the street and down through the lacy treetops to the small park in the square. She was particularly fond of this bit of green Pennsylvania countryside that was carefully cultivated in the heart of the city. All it lacked to make it perfect, she thought, was a fountain and the splash of water. Suddenly she had a nostalgic vision of the fountains in the Tuileries Gardens in Paris, where she and her younger brother, Gardner, had rolled their hoops when she was only seven. In all their travels in Europe when Aleck, her older brother, was studying in technical school in Germany, and after her brother Robbie had died there, the Cassatts had been drawn back again and again to Paris, that city beguiling to children and adults alike. They lived there for months at a time, so that it began to seem like home to Mary. While her mother and her older sister Lydia went shopping, and her father visited historic sites, she and Gard chattered in French with children playing *cache-cache* around the monuments in the Gardens. They sailed boats with them in the octagonal basin to the sound of the fountain splashing in the center.

Mary was eleven during their last long stay in Paris. That was 1855; the year of France's first world's fair when the whole city became a brilliant pageant. Bright flags, passenger balloons, and gay band music constantly floated on the air.

The Cassatts joined the throngs in the new Palais des Beaux-Arts, looking at the exhibit of paintings from all over the world. Mary did not remember the paintings themselves so clearly as she did the excitement they aroused. She could still see groups of Frenchmen wildly gesticulating in front of the paintings of Ingres and Delacroix, shouting such words as *"classique"* and *"romantique"* at each other. Mary's father could scarcely believe his eyes

5

and ears. "These Frenchmen!" he said. "Even the businessmen act as though the kind of art they want on their walls is as important as the stocks and bonds they buy. You would never hear this wild kind of talk from my friends in Philadelphia!"

Out of curiosity, the Cassatts dropped in at a pavilion next to the Palais where a rebel, an artist named Courbet, had defiantly set up his own show. His grim and realistic paintings of villagers at a funeral and of peasants breaking up stone were different from pictures Mary had ever seen before. "Look, they show real people," she said.

Certainly his paintings were different from the old masterpieces in the Louvre. On afternoons when her father and mother and Lydia dutifully spent a brief hour or two hurrying through some of the endless galleries of this treasure house, they kept losing Mary. She was always holding back to watch the students who had set up their stools and easels here and there to study and copy canvases they admired. Some of those art students were young ladies. One girl, she remembered, copying a Raphael with such concentration that she didn't even notice Mary looking eagerly over her shoulder, couldn't have been more than sixteen years old.

Sixteen! The thought of her birthday came over her afresh. If she herself could go to Paris now, Mary thought, she would haunt the Louvre every day. She would study masterpieces so closely that she would soon learn how to paint the way she really wanted to! Mary took a deep breath. And today was the day! The day she must get up her courage to tell the family that she had made up her mind. She was determined to become an artist. They would have to let her go to live and work in Paris!

Throughout the day, Mary waited for the right moment to break the news of her plan. That moment did not come until evening toward the end of the festive birthday dinner, with all the family gathered around the long mahogany table.

The traditional Philadelphia white mountain cake, towering high and ablaze with candles, was set down before Mary. She closed her eyes, made a silent wish, took a deep breath, and blew. Sixteen candles went out at once. But the seventeenth, the one to grow on, wavered, then flamed bright again.

Young Gard called out, ''Now your wish won't come true.''

Mary looked so crestfallen that her father laughed and said that the seventeenth candle didn't really count until next year. Gallantly he proposed a toast to his younger daughter, ''almost grown up now, a sweet sixteen.''

With all eyes on her, Mary felt the warmth of her family's deep affection for her, for each other. This, then, must be the moment!

Mary began, trying to tell them in a rush the hopes and plans that she had kept to herself for so long. She tried to tell them of her ambition to make something important of her talent, how she wanted to make art a career, to learn to paint so well that some day her family would be proud of her, that even strangers would buy her paintings and museums would hang her work on their walls.

Mary was so intent on getting it all said without being

interrupted that she tried not to heed the look of bewilderment in her mother's eyes or the growing look of incredulity and disapproval in her father's. A quick glance at the others around the table showed Lydia's startled face, Gard wide-eyed. Only Aleck was leaning forward and listening with sympathy.

Mary managed a smile. Resolutely she went on, looking at her father. "Since it is impossible for me to do all this at home, I want your permission to go live in Paris, where I can study seriously and become a professional artist."

By now her father was looking so stern that Mary tried to finish on a light, jesting note. "Instead of my just going off to Paris to live a new kind of life, you'd think I was going off to certain death."

Mary's father did not smile. For a long moment there was silence; then he said simply, "I would almost rather see you dead."

Mary gasped. The others looked startled. Her mother quickly held out her hand in an imploring gesture. "You don't mean that; you can't."

To make peace, Lydia said quickly, "Let's not spoil this evening by discussing Mary's plans now."

"But we must discuss them now," Mary pleaded.

"There is nothing to discuss," her father said. "It is unthinkable that any woman would propose to take up painting as a serious pursuit—and for money! Certainly no daughter of mine will be permitted to go off alone to Paris with such outlandish ideas."

Aleck spoke up. "But if painting is so important to her —" he began.

His father interrupted. "If Mary wants to putter around with her paints, she can continue to do so at home. Later on, if she wants to take art lessons, perhaps something can be arranged here at the Academy of the Fine Arts. But there is no great hurry about that. After all, she is barely sixteen."

Mr. Cassatt turned directly to his daughter and for the first time smiled. "Now, Mame, isn't it time to serve that birthday cake?"

Mary was as relieved as everybody else that the storm was over. Paris was still a long way off, but she had taken the first step.

CHAPTER II

One morning in 1861, seventeen-year-old Mary Cassatt walked briskly through the grassy courtyard of the Pennsylvania Academy of the Fine Arts, glancing only briefly at the familiar statue of Ceres under the huge hawthorn tree, hung now with the red haws of autumn. As she hurried up the wide marble steps, Mary was aware of a curious contradiction in her feelings. She was disappointed not to be in Paris as she had hoped. And the Academy wasn't the Louvre—far from it. Even so, it was exciting to be a full-fledged art student at last.

With the outbreak of the Civil War that previous spring, Mr. Cassatt had become more determined than ever not to let Mary stray far from home. In the new fall term, he decreed, it would be either the Academy or nothing for his ambitious daughter. Like most Philadelphians, he was proud of the graceful white edifice on Chestnut Street, often taking his family to see the public exhibitions there. Now that he was ready to allow Mary to enroll as a student, he was fond of reminding her that it was the oldest art school in the country.

"One of the most old-fashioned, too," Mary would counter. Once she even dared remind him how, in the early years, the Academy used to drape some statues on Mondays, ladies' day, so that female visitors would not be shocked at the sight of Greek and Roman gods and athletes. "Imagine the Louvre disfiguring art in that way!" she said. "But that was long before you were born," her father answered. "Things are different now. The Academy is much more modern." Mary hoped so.

Entering the rotunda, Mary smiled as she caught sight of the familiar statuary group, "Battle of the Centaurs." She remembered how, when she was much younger, she and her brothers Aleck and Gard had grown dizzy walking around and around the warriors, trying to distinguish the victors from the vanquished in their convulsive marble struggle.

In the galleries, old paintings gleamed softly in the dim light let in through the skylights above. Most of the oils were portraits of patriots or huge canvases of historical and allegorical subjects. Mary knew each of them well.

The pride of the Academy was Benjamin West's "Death on a Pale Horse," a vivid and frightening scene depicting the end of the world, crowded with rampaging horses and struggling, terrified people. When quite young, Mary real-

11

ized that after Charles Willson Peale, Benjamin West was Philadelphia's most famous painter. He had gone to England to study and was so successful that he became court painter to King George III and president of the Royal Academy in London. The Pennsylvania Academy made him an honorary member when it was founded in 1805.

Mary doubted that the Academy would ever make her or any woman an honorary member. They had never taken women painters seriously. And why should they, she admitted, when most women were content to decorate china or paint quaint scenes on glass or velvet! She admired "Death on a Pale Horse," but she had no ambition to paint anything so huge, so heroic, so awesome.

This morning she wondered fleetingly why one couldn't paint with skill something closer to home and to daily life. Something like Krimmel's "View of Central Square on the Fourth of July," for instance—an old painting of the very square on which the Cassatts' house faced. It was a pleasant scene of parents and children, some of them Quakers, enjoying the holiday. Now it was considered outmoded, but it had its own quiet appeal for Mary.

Today she did not linger over her few favorites but hurried on to join other new students in the room where the class in Artistic Anatomy was gathering for their first lecture by a professor from the Pennsylvania Medical University. An *écorché* or anatomical figure, a statue by Houdon imported from France, was used to demonstrate Dr. Thomas's discourse.

Muscles, bones, tendons—these were basic, he said. Every artist should be thoroughly acquainted with anatomy before he even tried to draw or paint. A human being was infinitely more than a face, more than skin and complexion, more than the color of eyes and hair. What makes a chin lift or a head turn? What makes an arm stretch or a back bend in a certain way?

Mary became absorbed, watching, listening, taking notes. In lectures and studies in the weeks and months that followed, she continued to make discoveries.

In drawing class, where plaster casts of ancient Greek and Roman statues were the models, the same anatomical principles were supposed to apply. But all the statues were frozen in classic pose. Copying them was easy for Mary. They could not breathe; they could not stir. Plaster casts were always plaster. Mary longed to be admitted to Life Class, where a few carefully selected men students could study, draw, and paint from a flesh-and-blood model. But there was no hope that a girl could be admitted to that advanced and privileged group. Propriety still forbade it.

By the second year, Mary and a friend of hers, Eliza Haldeman, were at the head of the class of young ladies in both drawing and painting. When Mary boldly announced that she intended to become an artist, Eliza followed suit. They were two who were serious, who worked hard. They thought that most of the others were rank amateurs, merely toying with pencils and paints and plaster, and were at the Academy chiefly to enjoy flirtations with young gentlemen students, who far outnumbered the young ladies.

One day Mary and Eliza discovered two of their classmates trying to make a cast of a gentleman's hand. He was a young doctor, not an art student. This was a personal project of two young ladies, definitely outside the curriculum.

When Mary and her friend Eliza walked in on them, things were not going well. The young man, with his hand properly greased and partially encased in plaster, was looking dubious, even anxious. The young lady who was attempting the molding looked flustered. What should she do next? As she introduced the visitor, she looked helplessly at Mary. She was obviously much relieved when both Mary and Eliza came to the rescue. Step by step they proceeded, properly finishing the molding, eventually removing it in two perfect halves, and finally spooning in the new plaster.

There was much light banter and laughter during each stage of the lengthy process. Finally, after carefully chipping off the shell with a chisel and wooden mallet, the artists revealed the finished cast—a perfect replica of the young doctor's hand. His ingenuous delight and gratitude amused Mary. And when he insisted on having a photographer take a group picture of all the participants, Mary stood demurely with the others, still wearing her long apron to protect her long full skirt, and holding her plaster dish and spoon.

Such frivolous diversions were rare inside the Academy walls. Mary disciplined herself in her studies even when she grew impatient with some of her instruction. By the spring of '62 she was considered one of the students who, according to the catalogue, were "sufficiently advanced in the practice of the profession, desirous of making studies in oils or water colors . . . from particular paintings belonging to the Academy."

*Mary Cassatt (extreme right) while a student at the Pennsylvania
Academy of the Fine Arts*

In March, Mary received permission to study and copy one of the heads from the enormous canvas, "The Deliverance of Leyden" by Wittkamp. She chose this Dutch painting in order to please her father, whose ancestor, Jacques Cossart, settled in Leyden after leaving France with other Huguenots.

Mary was still trying to prove to her father her determination to become a painter. But her hopes and plans of going abroad to study were submerged for the duration of the Civil War.

The Cassatts now lived in the country, in Chester County, making what had been their summer and weekend home into an all-year-round place. Mary loved the Pennsylvania countryside. Here they could all escape briefly from the city with its war factories and its hospitals, heartbreakingly crowded with the wounded. Here they could breathe fresh air. Mr. Cassatt neglected his brokerage practice in order to produce and harvest his own fruit and vegetables. The crops on too many farms went unplanted or unharvested from lack of help.

After a long day in the Academy at her easel or bent over a drawing board, Mary found it relaxing to romp with the dogs at home or ride one of the fine horses from the stable.

She was proud of her brother Aleck, who, after building the water wheel in the creek on the farm, bent his engineering skills to railroading. The problems of helping to transport men and supplies in wartime absorbed him.

Lydia and Mary and their mother knitted mufflers and rolled bandages for the soldiers. Mary and Gard found it difficult to concentrate on schoolwork, especially when battles raged not far to the south or as close as Gettysburg.

The war was everywhere. Where was art?

Mary found it in unexpected places—in *Harper's Weekly*, in *Frank Leslie's Illustrated Newspaper*. The only American artists who seemed to be producing anything for the public were the artist-correspondents. Most of them remained anonymous, but among them was Winslow Homer. He and the others went out to the camps, out on the fields of battle. They drew what they saw on the spot. As a skilled horsewoman, Mary was amused to see that, in the beginning, some of the inexperienced artist-reporters drew horses galloping with their feet out in front and behind, jumping like rabbits. But as the artist-reporters observed more and more at first hand, they began to draw horses running and rearing in battle as they really did. And they drew men in battle suffering and dying as they actually suffered and died.

When peace finally came, personal lives and careers that had been wrenched out of joint for four long years were once more painfully set in forward motion.

Now Mary Cassatt had proved to her father through her persistent pursuit of study at the Academy that she was still determined to become an artist. Once again she looked toward Paris. At last her father gave his consent. Mary might study abroad when and if proper arrangements could be made.

CHAPTER III

Throughout the long months when Mary's father corresponded with acquaintances in Paris, making inquiries and plans as to what he considered "proper arrangements" for Mary's life there, she was wise enough not to show her growing impatience.

She did not protest when finally, in the spring of '66, her parents and Lydia set sail with her in order to make sure their Mame was suitably and pleasantly settled. As their ship pitched and rolled most of the way across the wide Atlantic, reducing her to wretched seasickness, Mary remained undaunted. None of these things counted.

No matter, either, that when her family sailed for home, they left her enrolled in the almost too correct and fashionable atelier of the artist and teacher, Chaplin. They left her living in an almost too quiet *pension* ruled by Madame, the genteel landlady, and frequented by proper Philadelphians. But Mary had no real longing for the Bohemian life. She knew that one didn't have to live unconventionally or in a garret in order to work hard and paint well.

What did matter to Mary was that she was now in Paris. It was the month of May; the chestnuts were bright with blossoms. She was twenty-two, full of energy and delight and on her own at last.

Chaplin urged all his students to visit the annual Salon, the exhibition at the Palais de l'Industrie. "If you are ever going to amount to anything," he said, "you must paint so that some day you will be accepted there."

This was the place to see what was happening in the very center of the world of art. To be accepted by the jury for this huge annual exhibition, sponsored by the Académie des Beaux-Arts, meant everything to the young and unknown artist as well as to the old and famous. Receiving a medal or even honorable mention here meant international recognition and public commissions. Critics brought overnight success to a few by extravagant praise in the journals and at least notoriety to others by violent denunciation. Here, mingling with the artists themselves, were rich patrons ready to make purchases.

Mary's first visit to the vast halls of the Palais was an overwhelming experience. She saw hundreds, thousands of paintings in room after room. Altogether, four thousand paintings lined the walls, arranged from the desirable eye level up to the place of exile just under the ceiling. It was impossible to take them all in. Some day, Mary promised herself, she would have a painting of her own on these very walls.

On succeeding visits, sometimes alone, at other times with new art-student friends, Mary found that certain paintings began to stand out from those having the usual literary and historical themes. There was, for example, a contemporary portrait called "Two Sisters" by a Monsieur Degas. The portrait struck Mary because the artist apparently thought it important to have his models look real rather than pretty. As she studied it, Mary resolved to remember the name: Degas.

But the real sensation of the year was a painting called "Camille" by a M. Monet. Not the notorious *Manet* who the year before had scandalized the critics and the public with his startling "Olympia"—but *Monet*. This unusual portrait of his model ("His mistress, no doubt!" said the art students) with her back turned and wearing a shimmering green silk striped gown and fur-bordered jacket was striking in a way that brought cries of both admiration and indignation. The marvel was that it had been accepted at all. It was poorly hung high on the wall. But to Mary and scores of others, it shone with disturbing brilliance in an otherwise neglected dark corridor.

Mary went back several times, craning her neck to study it—the unconventional pose, the profile of the not very pretty face, the effect of opulence in the silken gown. She read with interest the high praise of Zola, the famous writer, newly turned art critic. He started off by saying, "The canvas that stopped me longest was the 'Camille' of M. Monet."

Back in her art classes under Chaplin, Mary found no such striking originality. Chaplin's painting was not only traditionally safe and sure but suave. He gave his students a few new technical tricks which a young painter could adopt in order to get quick, smooth effects. But that was all.

When Mary and the other young ladies in the class were sent to the museums, they were encouraged to copy such superficial paintings as Chaplin's own pretty and popular "Girl with Cat" in the Luxembourg.

This was no challenge to Mary. More and more she chafed under the limiting influence of one teacher. Suddenly she made up her mind to leave the studio and work independently. She would seek out other teachers. They would be the best; they would vary widely, coming from many countries, many periods, and many schools. They would be the masterpieces hanging in the Louvre. After all, that was what Paris had that Philadelphia lacked. And Mary remembered that Ingres, that classicist and master draftsman, had said that it was good to study the old masters, not in order to imitate (as many teachers mistakenly urged), but in order to learn to *see*.

Through the next few years Mary set up her easel for long hours at a time in different galleries of the Louvre, learning to see for herself, training her eye as well as her hand.

How had Prud'hon captured the magic of light and shade? How had the modern Corot put unbelievable nymphs in believable landscapes? How had the Dutch masters used windows and mirrors so effectively? How had the

"Art Students and Copyists at the Louvre" (*Winslow Homer*)

Venetian school developed such incredibly glowing colors? Did Titian's quick feathery brush strokes account for the richness in his textures? Mary was drawn back often to study Raphael's serene "La Belle Jardinière." Here the perfect Virgin was also the tender mother; the Babe and small saint were also real boys. How did the artist do it?

In those next few years Mary found it was easier to learn to see what the masters had done and even to understand a little of how they had done it than it was to do the same things herself. It was far easier to make a recognizable copy than it was to re-create a masterpiece on her easel in the Louvre.

But Mary kept at her independent studies with ardent persistence. Here in Paris no one seemed to think it odd or unusual that this tall, well-dressed, keen-eyed girl who spoke French with an American accent, spent so many hours hard at work in the Louvre. Few other girls in the galleries were so completely immersed in their work.

One dark-eyed young French woman, a Mlle Morisot, appeared rather infrequently, but she seemed to Mary to be more serious and far more talented than all the others. She was not afraid to set up her easel before the largest Veronese or the most difficult Rubens. Mary would have liked to know her better, but for the time being they merely exchanged cordial *bonjours*.

When Mary's eyes grew tired from concentrated scrutiny of a single painting, there was always the limitless canvas of the out-of-doors to turn to—the streets and gardens of Paris, where she walked with delight in all kinds of weather.

She watched the buildings turn pearl gray in the autumn rains. She bought hot fresh chestnuts to eat, holding them first to warm her hands in winter. She saw the Seine touched with rose in the spring sunsets, the plane trees leaning out toward the river, the busy bridges and boulevards enlivened with carriages, top hats, and parasols. She watched the children in their pinafores, romping in the parks just as she and Gard had done long ago. All this was a constant refreshment to the young artist, drained from hours of close study in the museum.

There were times when Mary felt discouraged and lonely. It wasn't easy to make new friends now that she didn't belong to a studio. She reminded herself that the French were considered indifferent to all strangers.

As she passed the cafés, Mary envied the spirited young men artists who could gather there in the late afternoon and hold vociferous debates that must have lasted far into the night. But since young ladies could not linger at the cafés or talk to young men without proper introductions, Mary would hurry on, usually content to return to her comfortable *pension*. There she would have a restoring apéritif, delicious dinner, and polite conversation with Madame and the pensionnaires over coffee in the small gilt drawing room.

CHAPTER IV

Some of Mary's evenings were very pleasant, even gay. Friends from Philadelphia arriving in Paris always looked her up. The young men just out of college on a trip to Europe were glad to escort this attractive intelligent girl from home to dinner and the opera, or to a new play at the Comédie-Française, or to hear Adelina Patti, the coloratura soprano who was all the rage. Mary enjoyed dressing up in her new Paris evening gown, pulling on her long kid gloves, taking her fan and her cloak, and stepping into a cab with her escort. He in turn was glad to be going out with this young American who knew the best places for dining and for entertainment and who could speak French almost as well as English.

Mary always kept in close touch with her family. Lydia

and her parents came to visit her and continued to come each year. There were long letters from home to read and to answer. Aleck, now a successful railroad superintendent, was courting the girl he later married, Lois Buchanan, a niece of former President Buchanan. Apparently Lois was rather shy of joining the closely knit Cassatt clan. For Aleck's sake, Mary was happy to send her best wishes and write welcoming letters.

Young Gardner, who had decided to go into banking, was always interested in Mary's animated accounts of her new life. Occasionally she sent canvases home to show her father that she was making progress in her work.

In 1867 there was a world's fair, brilliant reminder to Mary of the one she had seen in Paris as a child. This exposition, opening April 1 on the Champ de Mars, drew crowned heads from everywhere—Japan, Prussia, Turkey, Russia, Egypt, and Greece. There were public processions, concerts in the gardens, dancing in the streets, and galas every night. Mary thought that the start of each day was like watching the curtain go up on a new stage performance.

But Mary never let herself be diverted long from art. The *Prix de Rome* that year was given for the strong, narrative painting "Laius Killed by Oedipus." Most of the canvases lining the walls of the Salon also took their inspiration from mythology, history, or literature. Mary admired many of them and thought that some day she might attempt to paint an original interpretation of one of her favorite poems by Tennyson, "Mariana," but she did not feel ready yet to submit anything of hers to the jury.

Here and there, badly hung and almost lost among traditional subjects, were a few different kinds of paintings— those depicting ordinary contemporary life. A canvas that attracted Mary was "Paris seen from the Trocadero"— a quiet outdoors scene, fresh and delicate, with sketchy figures of two ladies and a small girl in the foreground of the sweeping and open composition. To her surprise and delight, she discovered that it was painted by her acquaintance from the Louvre, Mlle Morisot.

No scandalous or sensational painting had been admitted this year. Those of Monsieur Manet were so completely rejected that he, like Courbet long before, optimistically set up his own show of fifty paintings in a separate pavilion, hoping that the public would be more receptive than the jury. But most people just laughed at Manet's paintings.

Mary did not laugh, but she was startled by this artist's strange new approach. Here she saw for the first time the infamous "Olympia"—a pale nude, not at all like the rosy Venus of tradition. The nude was not modestly averting her gaze but was staring, unashamed, directly at the onlooker. The almost black background, the black face of the black woman delivering the bouquet, the black cat at the foot of the bed—all made a striking contrast with the nude and the creamy white of the pillows and bed coverings. Mary, trained to try for warm, rich colors and subtle gradations of light and shade, was taken aback by the stark flatness of the painting.

Other canvases in Manet's pavilion were almost equally disturbing. None of them told a story. The subjects were never idealized. Mary thought that most of his models must have been taken off the back streets of Paris, wearing their everyday shabby clothes: street musicians, alcoholics, gypsies. She studied them intently. Apparently Manet painted them just as he saw them, and his way of painting produced canvases that were different and so strange that people laughed because they did not understand them. She herself was not sure she understood or even liked Manet, but at least she was beginning to realize that the old ways of painting might not be the only ways. There were new and interesting ideas in the air. Still, Mary decided, she had much to learn of the old ways before she grappled with the new.

Toward the end of summer, when Paris was deserted by all who could get away to the mountains or the sea, Mary too was always ready for a change. In August of 1869, weary of city heat and airless museums, she and a friend, daughter of the Gordon family in Philadelphia, set out on a sketching trip. Mary privately thought her visitor a rank amateur as an artist, but she was good company and an ideal companion for this carefree excursion.

With a minimum of baggage, of which walking boots and sketching materials in knapsacks were the most important items, the two girls gaily boarded the train for the mountainous region near the Italian and Swiss borders. Stopping overnight in the town of Macon, they found the birthplace of the poet Lamartine, and a restaurant where they dined for the first time on delicious frogs' legs au gratin.

Aix-les-Bains, their next stop, was entirely too dressy for summer vagabonds who were not interested in spending their time in a fashionable casino. They found the opposite extreme in the mountains of Bauges, where they stayed in a farmer's small house until they discovered that, by taking the bedroom, they were exiling their hosts to sleeping in the straw in the barn.

Finally, the two American gypsies ended up in Beaufort on the river Doron in Savoy. Here they stayed in a roomier but still primitive farmhouse on the edge of the village. The region was wild and beautiful, the crystal-clear air was intoxicating, the views of the meadows and mountains were breathtaking.

The hearty meals were feasts to the hungry visitors: trout brought straight from the cold rushing streams, omelets made from the freshest eggs. Every simple dish was seasoned to perfection with herbs from the mountain meadows. The girls themselves picked wild berries for the family table. The cheeses from the region went perfectly with the fresh and fragrant Beaufort white wine.

When the two young artists started sketching in the neighborhood, they were soon surrounded by curious and friendly children. Adults, too, were fascinated and were happy, for a franc or two, to take a half hour from daily chores to pose somewhat self-consciously in their picturesque local costumes There was much giggling over the results, and much laughter over the attempts of the two American ladies to understand and to speak the mixture of French-Italian common to the region.

Sometimes the two girls set off on long walks up the mountain slopes. One day they walked for twelve hours, up the side of a nearby mountain and down again. On their

31

long climb they began to crunch along in ankle-deep snow until at the top they were rewarded by a magnificent view of Mont Blanc and the St. Bernard. How could one sketch such a panorama on a mere piece of paper! Somehow, even with cold stiff fingers, Mary did it, putting much into a few quick strokes of her pencil.

They thought that their picnic luncheon of bread, Gruyère cheese, and wine, with apples for dessert, tasted better than any meal they had ever had. When they reached the farmhouse again after the long descent, they devoured big bowls of hearty meat-and-cabbage soup that made them forget how tired they were.

Country life suited Mary. She went back to Paris all aglow, determined to have just such a vacation next year. But by the next August, 1870, France was at war with Prussia. Alarmed for her safety in Paris, Mary's family cabled that she must leave. And so, packing up most of her personal belongings and the best of her finished canvases, Mary sailed for home.

CHAPTER V

It was good to be home again in Philadelphia with her family, who were now living right in the city, though Mary made it clear that she would go back to Europe as soon as she could. When family friends twitted her about deserting her own country and preferring to live in France, she declared, "You know I am American and always will be! Some day, people like me who want to be artists will have everything they need to study right here. We'll have great public art collections in museums, and art schools that don't just try to imitate the most rigid academies of Europe. But until that day comes, I'll have to live and work abroad."

Her own family were loyal to their Mame and her ambitions, but occasionally Mary had to endure well-meant but awkward questions from others about her future. Though nobody said anything about her being almost twenty-seven years old, Mary knew the thought lurked behind every question. Wasn't she interested yet in getting married? Perhaps there was a Frenchman somewhere in the offing that she wasn't talking about? Wasn't she about ready to settle down and make a home for herself and a husband? Didn't she like children? Surely she didn't intend to spend the rest of her life painting!

Mary tried to laugh off the questions. She found that there was little use in explaining to these kind but conventional and curious people that, for the present at least, painting meant everything to her, that she had much to learn before she could think of another kind of life for herself.

She did protest that of course she liked children! It was wonderful to have a new young nephew in the family, Aleck's and Lois's two-year-old son, Eddie. She had started to paint his portrait and found him a completely charming, if wiggly, model. She was doing him in a rather formal eighteenth-century manner in red velvet suit and lace collar. But the results were disappointing. She sighed that she still had something to learn about richness of color. Other members of the family posed for her, too.

While the war dragged on in France, Mary grasped what news she could. She heard that paintings had been smuggled out of the Louvre and hidden from the enemy. Raphael's adored "La Belle Jardinière" had been taken from its frame and buried in a coffin-like box and sent away with other treasures—no one would say where.

"Alexander J. Cassatt and His Son, Robert Kelso Cassatt"
Mary Cassatt's portrait of her brother and nephew, 1884

Madame at the *pension* and other friends in Paris wrote of the siege of the city, how they were barely existing, without food or fuel, having to eat domestic pets and animals from the zoo. Mary shuddered over every letter. The city was bombarded; the cemetery of Montparnasse, the Left Bank, and the Latin Quarter were hit. If these anguished communications reached her at all, friends wrote, it would be because the letters had been sent out of Paris by balloon, and had safely reached a port.

Deeply distressed about the tragedy of her adopted city, Mary tried to keep from brooding. She went to Pittsburgh to visit her mother's relatives and then across the Ohio River to Allegheny, her birthplace. Both cities were smoky, windowsills covered with soft-coal soot. But there was something magnificent about those hills and deep mines, the surging railroads, and the new flaring steel mills. All these gave Mary a sense of pride in her birthplace and her state.

One or two of Mary's relatives in Pittsburgh were persuaded to sit for her, just as others had in Philadelphia. Of course she gave the finished portrait to the family if they seemed to like it, and they usually said they did. But Mary felt that she should be selling paintings to strangers somewhere, someone impartial, if only to prove to herself that she was a professional. But where?

Aleck, as a railroad man, knew Chicago well. He spoke of the city's fine merchants, of businessmen who were not only newly rich but ambitious and intelligent. Perhaps there, where she had no Cassatt connections to restrain her, she could actually sell some paintings. Why shouldn't she try? She could stay at the brand-new Palmer House. Aleck said he would give her an introduction to Potter Palmer, a growing force in Chicago. Mr. Palmer had recently married a spirited, elegant young woman, a Kentuckian of French descent. The young Mrs. Palmer might easily be interested in the work of an American who had studied and painted in France. And the new Palmer House was close to the Academy of Design. The Academy might give her some other valuable introductions.

Mary's Pittsburgh cousins, Minnie and Aleck Johnston, decided to go see Chicago with her. Mary packed up her best French canvases and a few of her most effective Parisian gowns and set off by train from Pittsburgh for this thriving American metropolis in the midwest, Chicago.

It was October 1871, an unusually dry and warm October. Tired from their trip, the three travelers settled into the comfortable and handsome Palmer House, opened only two weeks before. Mr. Palmer had been called East, so Mary's attempt to sell paintings would have to wait. For the weekend she would explore this exciting city.

On Saturday a fire lit the sky in the distance. Though the fire smoldered all day Sunday, Mary and her cousins were assured that it was under control. They went for a walk through the nearby park on the lake front, though the wind was too strong and the air too smoky for the visitors to take much pleasure in the scene.

That night Mary went to bed with shutters clattering against the windows. About midnight she was awakened by a banging on her door, the sound of running feet, and shouts of "Fire! Fire!"

There was no time for packing more than two small cases. There was no time for the paintings. They dressed and rushed to the street. The rest was a nightmare. Bells were ringing. Fire-engine steamers surged past, trying to quench or outrun and contain the flames. On all sides people shouted, shoved, swore. The night was as bright as day. Mary and her two cousins, with bags in each hand, struggled through mobs on the sidewalks, trying in vain to get a cab to the depot. As they pushed their way on foot, glowing cinders fell in showers on all sides. A giant bonfire blazed all over the southwest. Twenty blocks crackled and roared with flames.

Mary tried not to think of the precious canvases she had to leave behind at the hotel. People on the streets were struggling with more basic things like mattresses and blankets and birdcages. There were elderly invalids, carried on stretchers, or pulled along in carts, and crying babies. Every family was trying to take its most precious belongings. But where? They had no place to go. Their one idea was to get anywhere out of reach of the fire.

Mary was touched by the sight of a small boy, crying as he trudged after his parents. Around his neck was hanging the family treasure—a landscape painting, strung on its long wire as it had hung upon the wall. The heavy frame bumped against his shins at every step.

The whole scene was like something out of Dante's Inferno. The colors everywhere were unbelievable: raw crimson, pink and gold, blue, green, purple, and most vivid sulphur yellow. Mary thought she could never have mixed them on her palette.

39

Behind them the Palmer House was a flaming ruin. Ahead, at last, was the railway depot and the train that took the three of them out of the inferno back to Pittsburgh, where the only fiery glow was from prosperous mills and coke ovens. Then, on the Pennsylvania, "Aleck's railroad," Mary went back to Philadelphia, to peace and quiet. With her precious paintings in ashes, she would have to start all over again.

News from Paris was still unsettling. France's defeat by the Prussians was bitter, but the civil struggle that followed between the Conservatives and the Communards was even more bitter and far more bloody. It would take time for Paris to recover, slowly, painfully. No artist could work there now.

Mary decided to sail for Italy. She would try to study there, and perhaps in Spain. Then some day when the Salon was revived in Paris she must get up her courage to enter something of her own. Imagine a Mary Cassatt painting hanging on those famous walls!

CHAPTER VI

In Rome, Mary worked hard, but went on to find her greatest impetus in the sunlit town of Parma, studying Correggio. For the rest of her life she referred to this sixteenth-century artist as a "prodigious master." It was not only his incomparable chiaroscuro, his balance of light and shadow, that she admired. In the Camera San Paolo she delighted in his playful representation of children, naked and completely natural, called "putti."

Mary craned her neck to see in the dome these merry "putti" in their oval frames or roundels wreathed in greenery. There the children were frolicking, cavorting with each other and with animals. The great hounds of the huntress goddess Diana were their pets. A small boy flung one arm around a huge white dog while with the other hand he tickled its throat. Again, high in the dome, a child held aloft a stag's head in triumph. Were the two children up there in another roundel taking turns riding a long-suffering dog? There was no doubt whatever that the cherubic boy in a different frame was full of mischief, blowing his horn directly into another innocent's ear.

Mary began to realize that children in paintings need not be elegantly dressed or stiffly posed. An unself-conscious child caught in one of his endless variety of natural motions made a much better model.

Feeling the need of more direct instruction, Mary enrolled in the Art Academy of Parma, studying for a while with Carlo Raimondi. Under him she learned something of the graphic techniques, the methods of engraving, that she was to develop much later.

Meanwhile, she wanted to do more with her painting. Going to Spain, she found harsher light, deeper shadows, dramatic contrasts. There were marvelous masters to study in the Prado Museum in Madrid—Goya, El Greco, and the Flemish Rubens. In Seville she discovered the bullfight and the spectacle of dark-eyed ladies in brilliant shawls, proud Spaniards in somber black. Under the stimulus of the exotic Spanish scene, she now painted more boldly than she had dared to do in the softer atmosphere of Italy or France.

One of her Seville paintings, "During the Carnival," turned out to be so satisfying that she suddenly decided to send it to the Salon in Paris. Why not? It was the best thing she had yet done, and the Salon, now revived after the war, would be a real test. If she ever wanted to gain recognition, why wait?

Her picture was of three Spaniards—two women and a man on a balcony. One woman was leaning on the iron railing, looking down at the carnival in the street. The other dark-haired beauty was looking back over her fan at the man in the shadows of the background.

Hesitant about what her family would think of her exposing the name "Cassatt" to the eyes of critical strangers, Mary decided to sign her canvas "Mary Stevenson," using her middle name inherited from her grandmother. Mary felt very reckless as she packed up her painting and sent it off to Paris.

During the following days of suspense, Mary kept painting furiously in the daylight hours, but in the back of her mind was always that tantalizing vision of the forty members of the solemn jury in Paris, inspecting hundreds and hundreds of paintings, promptly dismissing most of them, arguing over many, accepting some, even occasionally voting a wildly enthusiastic "yes" by raising their tall hats on their canes. Would hers be considered, rejected, or accepted? Mary braced herself for disappointment.

When the notice came that she was among the accepted, Mary to her own surprise broke down and cried. She could scarcely believe it. Here she was, an unknown American accepted by the most demanding, the most powerful art jury in the world!

The first thing to do was to write home the good news. The next thing was to go to Paris herself to see her painting hung in all its glory. Would it be stuck off in a dark corridor somewhere? Or possibly placed so high under the ceiling that no one would notice it? No matter, it would be *there,* and listed in the catalogue.

And there it was: "# 1433 'Pendant le Carnaval' by Stevenson (Mlle Mary)." Moreover, her painting was not stuck off in the dump room; it was hung in a favorable position "on the line," at eye level.

Mary was elated but tried to pretend indifference. On her daily visits to the Salon, she would saunter into the crowded room where her painting was displayed. She would stand trying to look like a casual critic, gazing for a few too brief moments at the canvas signed Mary Stevenson. No one else paid any attention to her or to her picture. "Yes," she thought, "it is good. But I can do better than that. And I will."

Mary worked even harder, spending her time where art flourished, in France and other European countries, including Holland. Mary flourished, too. Gaining confidence in her increasing skill, she carefully chose a new painting from her studies in Spain to send to the Salon the next spring. This one, "Torero and Young Girl," showed a girl offering refreshments in a glass to a bullfighter. Mary knew that this painting was better than the one already accepted by the Salon. It had clearer color, light, and a freshness that she had not achieved before. It told a story that ought to appeal to the jury.

She hesitated only a moment before signing this canvas "Stevenson-Cassatt." Her family had been so surprised and impressed when she was admitted to the Salon before that she felt they would not object now to having the name "Cassatt" on display and in the catalogue. The second canvas was accepted, and Mary was jubilant, feeling that now she was well on her way to recognition.

Back in Paris for that season of 1873, she felt her elation

"Torero and Young Girl" (*Mary Cassatt*), *1873*

somewhat dampened. It was not only that again no one seemed to pay any attention to her own painting in the Salon but that she kept hearing rumors of rebellion among artists who were increasingly dissatisfied with the all-powerful jury.

One day when she was examining one of the prize-winning paintings, she heard an indignant snort from a young man standing beside her. "Why do they always give prizes to monstrosities like this scene of Babylon?" he asked. "And the prize winner over there, all those Danaïdes. It's just another grandiose painting from mythology. The same artists doing the same kind of thing year after year! The new artists haven't a chance."

"But Manet has one here this year," Mary protested. "Haven't you seen it?"

The young man snorted again. "Yes, but you notice it isn't one of his bold new paintings like 'Olympia' or 'Le Dejeuner sur l'Herbe.' He was careful to submit a popular and tame canvas like 'Le Bon Bock' showing a Frenchman smoking a long pipe and drinking his beer like a Dutchman."

Mary protested again. "But that is not tame; it is a highly finished painting in the Dutch manner. Extremely competent."

"So it is," the young man admitted. "The jury has nothing against competence. But it doesn't give medals to any except those who do academic subjects in the old approved manner. Look around you. Where are any new subjects done in a new way by other artists? Where is M. Degas, for instance? He isn't here. He doesn't exhibit here

47

any more because he is as scornful of the jury as the jury is of him. And he is right.''

"Degas?" Mary asked. "I remember a painting of two girls shown here before the war. Is that the same Degas?''

"There is only one Degas," the young man answered.

"Well, what sort of artist is he that he can afford to ignore the Salon? What kind of paintings does he do now? Where can they be seen? Where is this Monsieur Degas?''

The young man shrugged. "He went off last autumn to visit relatives in America. Of course he may be back by now. As for his paintings, they are indescribable. But his subjects are always new and the way he paints them is new. You will see them here and there. Just keep your eyes open.''

CHAPTER VII

One day, some time later, Mary stopped short in front of a little art shop on the Boulevard Haussmann. In the window there were displayed two most unusual pictures. They were striking informal scenes of modern life in Paris— one of the race track, the other of the ballet. Who had done them?

Mary pressed her nose against the windowpane. In the lower left-hand corner of the race-track scene and in the lower right-hand corner of the ballet was the same signature, simple but clear: "Degas."

So this was the man who ignored the Salon jury in such a highhanded way. And these were two of his new canvases. In them there was little trace of old academic formality, although his drawing was almost classic, so firm and decisive was it. Apparently, Mary thought, Degas admired and learned much from the old masters, just as she had tried to. But he did not imitate them. How fresh, how new they were!

Here was a scene of Longchamp, the Paris race course. The horses were not racing at the moment but were shown being paraded before the grandstand by jockeys in their bright silks. Off to one side, one could glimpse the bustle of people behind the iron grill fence and in the grandstand. In the distance, three factory smokestacks made punctuation marks against the sky. But the sleek, nervous horses were all-important in the scene. Mary recognized at once that here was a man who knew how horses really looked and moved in a tense moment before they burst into action.

Nothing could please her more, unless it was Degas's other canvas in the window—the one of ballet dancers. These young and agile creatures were not placed behind the footlights receiving flowers, applause, and adulation as Mary often saw them at the opera. Instead, the artist had caught them backstage in a casual but busy moment before rehearsal. A few of the dancers were pirouetting. Others were adjusting their shoulder straps, their bodices, tying their ballet slippers. The wardrobe mistress was sewing up what must have been a last-minute tear in the gauzy fluff of one costume. Most unexpected of all was a glimpse of dancers' legs coming down a circular iron staircase, silhouetted against the light from a long window. Degas had cut off the upper part of these figures by his frame, but Mary felt that in another instant they would enter into the activity in the foyer.

For a long time Mary gazed searchingly and with delight at these two paintings. No wonder that the Salon would not accept Degas's work. His characters were not historic, they were not dramatic, they were not even posed. They were very much a part of modern Paris and were caught in those fleeting moments that come just before action.

When Mary finally tore herself away from the window, she couldn't help wondering about the man, Degas. What was he like? He seemed to know a great deal, not only about art, but about people. Mary thought he might even know too much about women and what they were like in their dressing rooms and in their unguarded moments. It might be disconcerting to meet Degas the man. But the artist, that was another matter!

Mary watched eagerly for more of his work as it appeared from time to time in the art-shop window, and she talked about it to anyone who would listen.

One such person was an American girl, Louisine Elder, who was polishing her French and eagerly soaking up music and art while attending a *pensionnat,* a private boarding school, directed by Mme Del Sarte, a friend of Mary's.

Mary, pleased with such an enthusiastic art devotee, took her to new exhibits and showed her the latest Degas when it appeared in the shop window. It was a pastel this time, ''Ballet Rehearsal,'' with the magic signature ''Degas'' in the upper right-hand corner. At first Louie, as her friends called her, wasn't at all sure that she liked it. ''It's strange and different,'' she said.

But as the two Americans leaned their foreheads against the windowpane, Mary enthusiastically pointed out the picture's new and attractive features. How masterfully the artist handled the difficulties of perspective and planes! How unexpected the point of view was, as though the painter were looking up from the orchestra pit at the stage. There the scenery was blue and shadowy in the background. The footlights shone on the ballerina poised in her studied position, *sur les pointes.*

Off to the left, other dancers fluttered like butterflies around old Jules Perrot, the *maître de ballet.* One girl deliberately turned her back to the front of the stage, leaning over to tie her slipper. On the right, like a black exclamation point sliced lengthwise in half, the orchestra leader stood, coolly observing. Finally, there was just a glimpse of one pointed slipper on the foot of a dancer about to step into view.

It was an exciting pastel. Mary made it sound even more exciting with her enthusiastic and astute commentary. As a result, Louisine Elder decided that this was a work of art which she had to have—no matter what it cost. With Mary at her elbow, she walked into the shop, asked the price, and promptly emptied her purse, putting five hundred francs into the hand of the astonished dealer.

As the two rode back to the *pensionnat* in a hansom cab, Louisine's gray eyes shone as she held tight to the new treasure in her lap. She chattered gaily with Mary, saying it was lucky that she already had her season tickets to the opera and the ballet because now she would have no more spending money for a long time to come. She would have

"Ballet Rehearsal" (*Edgar Degas*)

to postpone the new gown she planned to have made at her dressmaker's and forget that new beribboned bonnet at the milliner's. She would even have to give up for a while going to Rumpelmayer's for tea and all those heavenly *petits fours* they served every afternoon. Then she laughed, saying she did not mind in the least now that she had this luminous treasure, this Degas, to put on the wall of her room and cherish forever.

She couldn't hope to be a painter like Miss Cassatt, she said, but she could learn a lot from her about art. And maybe some day she could buy another painting. Mary was delighted with this seventeen-year-old's enthusiasm and talked eloquently about how important, how necessary, collectors were to artists and to art. Who could tell! This Degas pastel might be just the beginning of a fine collection for her! Mary beamed, thinking that her friend already had the flair of the true collector.

CHAPTER VIII

Seeing Degas's extraordinary work of ordinary people—
ballet dancers, jockeys, and sometimes even laundresses,
all in their workday surroundings, gave Mary's own painting a new direction. She began to ask herself why she
should try to paint stories like Tennyson's "Mariana,"
for instance. Mariana was not real; she belonged to the past
and to poetry, not to the present and to painting. Or why
should she even continue to paint bullfighters? They belonged to Spain; they were not part of Paris or of her
own daily life. Mary began to look around her, finding subjects in familiar faces, friends, and family when they came
to visit.

The following spring of 1874 she decided to submit to
the Salon again. Unlike Degas, she had no other place to

"Portrait of Madame Cortier" (*"Ida"*) (*Mary Cassatt*), 1874

exhibit; she had no picture dealer, no art shop interested in her work. But this time her Salon entry was different. It was not of romantic Spanish figures, but a forthright portrait of a woman, "Ida," Mme Cortier, who was neither young nor pretty. Instead she was middle-aged, had reddish hair and a cheerful, intelligent face, which Mary painted with candor, developing flesh tones with broad brush strokes.

Looking critically at the finished canvas, Mary thought that even Degas might approve. She had so much faith in her newly directed talent that for the first time she signed the canvas boldly and simply "Mary Cassatt."

While she was waiting in suspense to hear the verdict, Mary learned of a much smaller and livelier exhibition that opened April 15. The newspaper critics were having a great time poking fun at it. When Mary saw that Degas and Monet were listed as leaders in the show, she hurried over to see for herself. Eagerly she climbed the large staircase from the Boulevard des Capucines up to the second-floor studios loaned to the group by the photographer Nadar.

Here she saw paintings so alive that they made the dark red-brown walls shimmer with light and color. Going from room to room, Mary drank in all of the pictures. To her they were like champagne, sparkling, effervescent, intoxicating.

A group stood in front of the paintings by Monet, laughing and pointing. One canvas, "Boulevard des Capucines," was full of the atmosphere and the animation of people and carriages at carnival time in the very street below.

"Just look at those small black painted dabs," said a man next to Mary. "They're supposed to be people. People! They're just 'tongue-lickings,' that's what they are. I for one never look like that walking along the boulevard. Do you?" He suddenly turned to Mary, smiling broadly.

Mary's back stiffened. She realized that the man was just quoting what one of the critics, Louis Leroy, had said in the paper. She couldn't resist answering briefly, "I might look like that to an artist painting from an upper window. And so might you."

The man stared in astonishment at Mary; then quickly moved on.

In front of Monet's "Impression: Sunrise," another group was chattering and laughing. The only definite shape in the picture was the red-orange disk of the sun. Reflected in gently rippling water, it shone brilliantly in a broken path of orange-red, just the moment before its color would dissolve in the light of day.

"*Oo, la la,* what a sunrise!" said a fashionably dressed young lady. "Is that what they look like? I must confess I am never up early enough to know. I think the painter must have been sinking in the river when he tried painting that. It is more impression than sunrise."

"I heard one of the critics call Monet an 'impressionist,' " said her escort. "Isn't that *drôle?*"

Mary kept still. She knew that the term was meant to be insulting. "Actually, it's not a bad description," she thought, as she went on to look at other paintings. "Most of these artists are trying for just that—to give a vivid impression of how a scene looks in a fleeting moment before the sun shifts, the light changes, or the shadow moves."

60

"Boulevard des Capucines" (*Claude Monet*)

Mary saw vibrant landscapes painted by artists whose names she did not know—like Pissarro and Cézanne. Here, though, was a familiar name, Mlle Morisot, her acquaintance from the Louvre. She was the only woman in the show and had dared to desert the Salon to appear here. Mary admired her courage. She particularly liked the delicate and airy scene called "Cache-cache" where a mother and small child played hide-and-seek in the ambiance of a fresh summer day in the country.

Nearby, people were making fun of a ballet dancer by Renoir because he had given her "cottony legs." Mary did think that Degas's dancers were truer to life. Ah, here was the room to linger in. Degas had ten paintings and pastels. For Mary, Degas combined the best of the old with the best of the new. There was something reassuringly substantial and steady about his pictures that kept them from floating off in the way that some of the other canvases threatened to. Perhaps one could have too much champagne? Mary recognized again Degas's vigorous basic drawing and his unusual compositions that always made his subjects fascinating—even a blowsy laundress pressing down hard with her iron on a steaming ironing board.

Mary went back day after day to study Degas and this entire exhibition of color and light, paying no attention to the critics and crowds who chattered of "messy compositions, thin washes and mud splashes" and "these poor fools who daub."

Meanwhile, news that her own entry, the portrait of Ida, Mme Cortier, had been accepted by the Salon pleased her but gave her spirits less of a lift than she had expected. Oh, it was always an honor to be shown in the sacred halls of the Salon. But Mary thought somewhat wistfully of that small group of artists, those "Impressionists" who dared to do new things independently of the jury and who were loyally defending each other against all those critics who did not understand what they were trying to do. Here in the Salon, Mary was just one of the thousands. Who would ever notice?

Actually, Mary's rather small but bold canvas of the head of Mme Cortier did draw favorable comments. She even overheard a few. But the comment that would have meant most to her was one she did not learn of until much later.

Degas himself paused before her painting one day, attracted by its direct frank portrayal, done with much skill and no flattery. He said to a companion, the painter Tourny, "That is real. There is someone who feels as I do." As Degas glanced at the signature, he said in surprise, "A woman!"

Tourny nodded. "I think that is the American I met briefly in Antwerp when we were both studying Rubens there. As you see, she has a real gift. And I know she works harder than most women painters."

Degas studied the canvas with new interest and made it a point to remember the name: Mary Cassatt.

The following year Mary sent two portraits to the Salon. One was accepted. But the one she thought more interesting, more exciting, was a new picture of her sister Lydia, painted during a recent visit. It was promptly rejected. This was a shock. Was it because the colors were too bright? Perhaps the Salon saw and disapproved of the fact that she was influenced by Degas's work and the much ridiculed Impressionists?

Indignant, Mary decided to test the jury. She deliberately darkened the background of Lydia's portrait to make it more conventional, more academic. When she resubmitted it the following spring, it was promptly accepted. Mary was disillusioned. She had heard other artists grumble that the jury was narrow-minded and prejudiced against anything new, especially by an unknown. Now she believed them. She wished she would never have to depend on the Salon if what they accepted was her second-best.

If only she could meet some of the Impressionists! She obviously could not seek them out and introduce herself. No young lady, especially a foreigner, could take such a bold step. And she couldn't imagine an artist like Degas or Monet showing an interest in an unknown American. Mary cringed at the idea of approaching her idols and of being snubbed by them. Besides, they were scornful of all artists who exhibited at the Salon.

But if she did not show in the Paris Salon, where? Philadelphia? At her family's urging, she sent three paintings back to the Pennsylvania Academy for an exhibition. Philadelphia was polite about her work, but Mary strongly suspected that the politeness was because of her family and not the paintings.

If her homeland remained indifferent and the Salon continued to reject her best work, where else could she turn? Mary did not know. But she was resolved not to do second-best for anyone.

CHAPTER IX

Soon Mary faced another problem. Should she encourage her family to come to live in Paris? Her parents and Lydia were thinking seriously of such a move. Her brothers Aleck and Gardner were well established now in business at home. Her father wanted to retire early, and his reduced income would go much further in France, where living was so much cheaper. Their annual vacation trips to see her were too tiring and too expensive for such short visits.

Besides, they wrote, they wanted to end this long separation. Lydia wasn't well; she missed her sister. They all missed their Mame. Since she wouldn't come home to live, what would she think of their coming over there to live with her?

Mary, who was devoted to her family, was delighted at

the prospect and said so, but she had qualms about their possible demands on her time. She tried to warn them that her work took most of each day.

That was another thing, they said. They worried about her health, about her working too hard. Didn't she do anything except paint and go to exhibitions? Didn't she have any social life? Perhaps it would do her good to have her family there to take her away from her studio from time to time.

After that, Mary took care to write in detail about all her activities. If they came to stay, she said, they would see that her work always came first but she did take time off in the evenings. She assured them that in her own modest apartment she entertained occasionally, at tea or dinner, a few good friends whose conversation was lively and stimulating. They talked not only of art but about everything from French politics to Zola's latest novel.

She wrote that they mustn't worry about her health. She walked a great deal. On fine days she sometimes changed from her paint-spattered smock to her riding habit and went for a canter along the bridle paths of the Bois on a spirited horse rented from nearby stables. And, she said, if they came over to live, they would certainly all go occasionally to the races at Longchamp. At least she and her father would go. Her mother and Lydia might prefer to attend the brilliant performances of ballet and opera in the new opera house.

When her mother worried about Mary's wardrobe, Mary described to her and to Lydia her modish new evening gown of shirred silk. She had worn it when she, with all of Paris, had turned out to hear the golden voice of Sarah Bernhardt as Doña Sol in Victor Hugo's *Hernani*. Mary added, however, that if rumors of the star's wildly unconventional private life were even half true, Mme Sarah scarcely deserved to be called *"la divine"* when she was offstage.

Mary wrote about being highly entertained recently by a clever, good-humored new comedy, *La Cigale*. The hero played the part of an Impressionist painter whose paintings were just as good upside-down as they were rightside-up. Even Mary, who would hear no criticism of the Impressionists, thought it was very funny. Degas had done a sketch for the studio scenery in the play.

In other letters Mary said that she was seeing two American artists, expatriates like herself. Her family would enjoy meeting them. One was young John Singer Sargent, who had entered the ultra-fashionable studio of Carolus-Duran. (Imagine the pretension of a man who changed his name from Charles to "Carolus"! Mary wrote.) She liked Sargent but was afraid he was interested only in painting portraits of the rich and important.

James McNeill Whistler, who divided his time between London and Paris, came to call on her, too. Mary was amused at Whistler's foppish attire, his monocle, his long stick, and his Bohemian behavior as though, she said, he were defying his Puritanical mother and his rigid Westpoint background. She couldn't help laughing when she heard that Degas, who was full of *bons mots,* had said, "My dear Whistler, you behave as though you have no talent!" But Mary recognized how unusual his work was in tone and mood and she advised Louisine Elder to add some of Whistler's pastels to her growing collection.

"Self Portrait" (*Edgar Degas*)

And so the letters went back and forth until the decision was made. Her parents and Lydia would be coming to France to stay just as soon as her father could sell their house in Philadelphia and settle all his affairs there.

They would try not to interfere with Mary's work. She should keep her studio, of course. But would she please start looking for an apartment large enough for them all to live in comfortably? Not too expensive and not in a fashionable *quartier,* but of course in a neighborhood that was perfectly respectable.

They would be pleased to meet her artist friends such as Sargent and Whistler. And had she met M. Degas yet? Mary replied briefly that, no, she had never met Degas. She did not say that the more she heard about his personality, the less sure she was that she wanted to meet him. He was proud and rude, people said. A confirmed bachelor, he hated women. It must be so, they said; look at the way he draws his models—in the most awkward and ungraceful positions, yawning and scratching, struggling to comb their hair, and even having their toenails trimmed!

Degas kept pretty much to himself. Occasionally he insulted even his few friends, and he was brutally frank with everyone. The younger artists were shocked at his remark to an admiring student who asked to be introduced to Degas in a shop. When Degas asked him who had painted a certain picture he was trying to sell, the young man proudly admitted that he himself was the artist. Degas merely commented, "I feel sorry for you," and turned his back on the boy.

Mary had always admired Degas the artist. Now, in spite

of what she heard, she began to be intrigued by what she knew of Degas the man. He sounded independent, to say the least. Well, she was independent too, and she would not be afraid of him, but certainly she was not going to seek him out.

In the end, it was Degas who sought her out. One day when Mary answered a knock at her studio door, she recognized her old acquaintance of Antwerp days, M. Tourny. Beside him stood a rather handsome man, with neatly trimmed beard, looking directly at her with dark searching eyes under heavy lids and raised brows.

M. Tourny greeted Mary, then went on, "May I present to you, Mademoiselle Cassatt, my friend, Monsieur Degas, who has long wished to make your acquaintance."

That afternoon was one of pure enchantment for Mary. Tourny, who made his living copying old masters, hovered in the background. Degas insisted on seeing everything that Mary had been doing—oils, pastels, sketches. He grasped at once what she had been trying to do in each instance. Occasionally he made a quick suggestion as to a line, a composition, but for the most part he was full of enthusiasm and admiration. "These are real," he said. "Most women paint pictures as though they were trimming hats. Not you!" Mary glowed with pleasure at his praise.

At the end of the afternoon Degas began to reveal the purpose of his visit. He told Mary how much he had admired her portrait of Mme Cortier three years ago at the Salon. He had also noticed her more recent entries. Did she plan to continue to show at the Salon? Perhaps, on the other hand, she was aware of the group of independents who called themselves Impressionists?

Mary merely nodded, not daring to interrupt. Degas went on to say that he did not really approve the name "Impressionist." But whatever they called themselves, they were still called lunatics by the press, even this past spring at their third showing. He realized that to ally one-self with such a group might take courage. But, he said, looking directly at Mary, it struck him that Mlle Cassatt was an artist with that kind of courage.

Then he came to the point. Would she consider joining the Impressionists? They needed her. Most important of all, her work was such that they would be proud to have her exhibit with them the next time they had a showing, possibly next spring.

Throughout this long speech Mary's eyes had never left the face of this man who was so unexpectedly handing her the answer she had been looking for—the answer to her work, perhaps her entire future. After a moment's silence Mary said simply, "Thank you. I accept your invitation." Then, because that seemed completely inadequate to this momentous occasion, she added in a rush, "I accept with joy."

There was handshaking and plans to meet soon again. Perhaps, Degas said, Mademoiselle would care to come to his studio and look at his work? M. Tourny would be happy to escort her there. Usually, Degas said, he admitted his few visitors only at the end of day when the working light had faded. But Mademoiselle would be welcome at any time. Perhaps tomorrow afternoon? Good!

There was more handshaking and there were *au revoirs*. As Mary closed the door after her two callers, her thoughts were in a tumult. She was jubilant over having a place at last to show all her best work—not just one or two things that the unpredictable Salon jury might not even accept. And she was elated over the approval of the great Degas. Could this sensitive artist, this charming man, possibly be the disagreeable Degas who hated women?

CHAPTER X

That visit to Degas was exhilarating and the first of many for Mary. His studio, only a short walk from hers near the Place Pigalle, became almost as familiar to her as her own.

On this first day she looked around eagerly. The studio seemed to be overflowing with clutter, but Mary soon realized that every bit of it was useful to Degas. A large stuffed horse was most startling. This and many small wooden horses with movable legs were easy to manage and helpful when Degas tried to recapture certain positions of horses on the race course.

Mary saw his collection of ballet frocks, slippers, and ribbon sashes, kept there for models from the ballet school. There were Japanese prints and fans, showing his interest in the art of the Orient. There was a plaster nude, full-size, given him by a sculptor friend. There was a special camera, for Degas had become an enthusiastic photographer. Photographs large and small were scattered in heaps about the room. There was a standing mirror which could be tilted to supply the surprising and unexpected angle.

Everything seemed somewhat dusty and in disarray—everything except his paints and his canvas on the easel, which at the moment was "L'Absinthe," posed for by two friends in the café. Mary realized afresh that there was no dust or disarray in this artist's keen mind.

In the weeks that followed, as she watched Degas paint or listened intently to his forthright criticism of her own work, Mary felt that at last she had found the school, the master she could respect. Degas would not permit her or anyone else to call him *"maître."* He had no pretension about him and was scornful of those who had. He was free with advice and criticism, sometimes to a point that stung. Mary began to see why people thought him rude, even cruel. She learned to brace herself, taking his criticism when she agreed with it, but daring to argue with spirit when she was sure of her ground. He was generous with enthusiasm and encouragement, too, and that made it all worthwhile. Their meetings in each other's studios became the high points in Mary's life.

But these were interrupted when Mary's family arrived in Paris to live in 1877, when Mary was thirty-three. The Cassatts busied themselves with moving together into the larger apartment Mary had found in the same *quartier,* Montmartre, near her studio. Mary was torn between the

"Mary Cassatt at the Louvre" (*Edgar Degas*)

domestic pleasures of having her family around her and fears that her work would suffer just when it seemed more important than ever.

After the first flurry of redecorating and furnishing the apartment with a mixture of some old favorites brought from Philadelphia and new purchases in Paris, Mary's family agreed that she should go back to her daily routine of work. They understood, they said, that she wanted to take advantage of the help and advice of Degas. They knew how important it was for her to get ready to exhibit with the Impressionists in the spring.

Mary had undertaken a self-portrait and was having difficulty with the tilt of her head under its flowered bonnet, the angle of the pose, and the composition as reflected in the mirror. Degas helped her to solve her difficulty. Sometimes they went to the Louvre together to refresh their memories of how an old master had solved certain problems in his day. Mary had never enjoyed museums so much as she did in the company of this fascinating man.

The two of them became a familiar sight in the Louvre: Mary's slender, erect figure, walking briskly down the corridors beside Degas with his somewhat rounded shoulders and rolling gait. Mary's intense concentration as she stopped to study a canvas led Degas to say he must paint her in just that pose some day. Even her back reflected that concentration. He began to make quick sketches of her there and then.

Gradually Mary met all the Impressionists, who welcomed her as one of them. Degas introduced her, too, to Durand-Ruel, who showed interest in becoming her dealer.

She felt happily that life was opening wide for her, spreading out like the Japanese fan which Degas had given her.

As Mary saw more and more of Degas, she was struck and pleased by how much alike they were in many ways. Degas, now in his early forties, was ten years older than she, but they looked at things in the same way. Once, when someone spoke of art as a luxury, Degas said firmly, "Art is not a luxury but an absolute necessity." Mary agreed. Art was as necessary to her as breathing.

Another time he said to Mary, "There's nothing very hard about painting when you haven't gone into it. But once you have, that's quite another matter." Each recognized that the other had "gone into it" passionately with both mind and heart. They had the same tireless drive for work: work so absorbed them both that it was only gradually that Mary learned about Degas's personal life and background. Even these facts proved to be somewhat like her own. She learned that Degas's father had been a banker, a cultivated man, fond of music, and not much interested in business.

"Like my father," Mary said, telling of her father's early retirement so that he could enjoy life in Paris.

On the other hand, Degas's brothers were more interested in banking and business than in the arts. "Just like Gard and Aleck," Mary said.

Degas's family had hoped he would go into law, but he persuaded them that art was all he cared about. Mary nodded in understanding, telling him of her own declaration of independence.

She gathered that the DeGas family had fallen into some

dreadful sort of financial difficulty which Degas never fully explained, although it was obvious that he was exercising strict economy in order to help pay off some family debts. She concluded that his family was an old one—respected, even important—and that they were proud of the name which they still spelled *DeGas*. But they didn't give a sou for society as such. And Degas himself not at all. In fact, he was so irritated by the old aristocratic spelling of the family name that he deliberately used the simpler form.

"The Cassatts are all proud of our name," Mary said, but added that her parents avoided socialites, those Americans who in Paris were interested only in being seen in all the fashionable places, wearing the latest and retelling the latest gossip.

Of course Mary often wondered why Degas had never married. Like everyone else, she had heard him quoted as saying, "I would be in misery all my life for fear my wife might say, 'That's a pretty little thing,' after I had finished a picture."

Mary thought with amusement that Degas would never have the courage to say such a thing directly to her. He must know by now that she could never make such a stupid remark.

Mary soon decided that he really liked women, but—possibly in self-defense?—he pretended to be scornful of them, their frivolities, their conversation. Oh, women were pretty to look at, he admitted—and sometimes as graceful as horses in motion—but most of them chattered incessantly about nothing. Their bonnets made handsome designs and he liked to see them in the shops and on their pretty heads.

He liked, for instance, the bonnet which Mary was wearing as she painted her own portrait. It was abloom with ribbons and flowers. But artificial flowers were the only kind of blossoms he liked. He couldn't abide real flowers in a garden, on a dinner table, anywhere! They smelled so! That was one reason he couldn't stand the country.

Mary protested. She adored flowers. Bringing home bouquets from the flower markets of Paris was one of her pleasures that made winter in the city apartment attractive. The scent of carnations or roses brought up to the city from the South of France was to her the most delicious of perfumes.

Degas snorted. Perfume! That was another thing. Women were always drenching themselves in perfume. Mary laughed. She did not point out to him that she never drenched herself in perfume. As for "incessant chatter," it was obvious to her that Degas enjoyed her conversation —perhaps because it was seldom trivial and could be as pointed as his own.

Still, Mary wondered if a man with Degas's sharp tongue wasn't easier to work with than he would be to live with. He had old Zoé, his *bonne,* his housekeeper, to look after him. He didn't seem to need anyone else. Zoé even read the newspapers to him so that he could save his failing eyesight for painting.

Degas's evenings were apparently spent at the café within sound of the fountain in the Place Pigalle. Here he found the congenial company of other men—artists like Manet and Renoir and Pissarro; writers like the Irishman George Moore, and a few critics. They argued for hours over cigarettes, coffee, and their glasses of beer. The group had

"Reading Le Figaro"
A portrait of her mother by Mary Cassatt, 1883

their own marble-top tables there in the Nouvelles Athènes, where the ceiling was adorned by the picture of a large dead rat. They argued until the metal shutters clanged up over the glass front at closing time.

Mary sometimes wished she could join them, but the café was a man's retreat and refuge where ladies did not intrude. Mary saw from the sketches Degas brought back that women of the streets sometimes sat at the tables by the windows, idle, quarrelsome, and expectant. Did he just sketch them? Or did he sometimes follow one home? Mary did not want to know.

Mary's retreat and refuge after a long day at her studio was the comfortable apartment where her family welcomed her with warm affection and a simple but delicious dinner, beautifully prepared and served, when they weren't entertaining old friends from Philadelphia or going out to a restaurant before the ballet or opera.

One evening, when they had all settled down to a quiet evening *en famille,* Mary settled into her own chair and began to sketch under the lamplight. She tried to catch precisely the characteristic pose of each one of this group of familiar and willing models. There was Lydia, frail and graceful, reclining on the chaise longue, taking up her sewing, making a ruffle on a new blouse for Mary. Her mother sat upright in the flowered chair, reading the news in *Le Figaro.* Her father leaned back comfortably in the largest armchair, from time to time peering over his glasses to tell them of some fascinating bit of French history from the book he was reading.

Later, when the others started for bed, Mary stepped out

through a long window onto the balcony, took a deep breath of mild night air, and leaned on the iron railing. For a long time she looked dreamily out over the rooftops of Paris and down into the street seven stories below where gas lamps bloomed soft yellow in the night.

She thought that at night Paris, blurred and mysterious, was just like an Impressionist painting, full of elusive magic. When two men on the sidewalk passed quickly through the soft yellow circle of light, Mary saw them as brief strokes from a brush dipped in black.

"People look just as Monet saw them from his upper window," she thought, "even if critics do call them 'tongue-lickings.'"

Mary smiled, remembering that it wouldn't be long now until she would be exhibiting with Monet and Degas and the others. Would the critics make fun of her, too?

CHAPTER XI

In this early spring of 1878 Mary waited impatiently, not only for the annual miracle of bright flowers in the parks and gardens, but also for the fresh miracle of seeing her own works bloom on the walls of the Impressionist Exhibition—their fourth, her first.

She was bitterly disappointed. At a gathering of the Impressionists in late March to discuss plans, it soon became evident that there were many obstacles in the way of any group showing. First of all, a new world's fair was to open in May in Paris, presenting a tremendous international art exhibit. Thousands of visitors coming to Paris for the fair would, as a matter of course, go to see the conservative exhibit there because of its prestige.

Durand-Ruel, whose gallery the Impressionists might

have used, had decided instead to have a showing of the more dependable and renowned masters like Delacroix, Courbet, Millet, and others of the Barbizon School.

Even if they could rent another place, it was doubtful that anyone would come to look at the Impressionists this year, not even to laugh. All were discouraged. They spoke of the widespread depression in France. Unconventional art was the last thing people would spend money on. Look at the disgracefully low prices offered to the Impressionists this past year! It was almost better not to try to sell at all.

Mary listened with a sinking heart. Her personal disappointment was great enough, but she was becoming sadly aware of the very real hardship that most of these painters were facing. The other woman in the group, the charming Mlle Morisot, who was now Mme Manet, having married the artist's brother, was in no critical financial danger. Nor was Mary. Both had families to rely on if their paintings did not sell.

But Degas, even though he sold more than the others, was strapped for money because of the family debt he was trying to pay off. The landscape artists could scarcely buy enough bread and wine or even artists' materials to keep going. Often they had to scrape off a finished painting in order to use the same canvas over. They tried to laugh, but the bitterness came through.

Some, like Pissarro and Cézanne, were so desperate that at times they were tempted to give up painting altogether. Others, like Monet, had swallowed their pride and begged for help from anyone who would take paintings in return for rent.

Renoir reluctantly decided that his only way out was to send to the Salon again. There he would at least be seen by the public and a buyer might turn up. Perhaps, after all, Manet was right in never having left the Salon.

It was obvious to Mary that the group hadn't the heart or the means to undertake a show this spring. Things couldn't get worse, they said; perhaps they would get better. Then they could try to have an exhibition next year.

Mary, their newest member, looked around at these artists with admiration and sympathy, feeling a fresh surge of indignation toward the hostile or indifferent public that had reduced them to such a state of discouragement. She had been so involved in her own work and in Degas's that she had not been fully aware of the plight of the others. Certainly their paintings, so full of sun and *joie de vivre,* gave no hint of their financial worries. She was resolved to do what she could to help them and to express her confidence in them and their work.

She had already bought a couple of irresistible ballet and theater pictures from Degas. Now Mary began quietly to buy a canvas here, another there, as she could afford to, from the other Impressionists. She became eloquent on their behalf to her American friends, not only Louisine Elder but others who had taste and more money to spend. They bought paintings, not from any sense of charity, but because of Mary's passionate conviction that the Impressionists had the most worthwhile modern art to be found in France. It would be good, she argued, to take this kind of painting back to America—good for Americans to be among the first to recognize these artists who would some day be appreciated by their own shortsighted countrymen. Besides, she would add shrewdly, "If you are looking for a fine investment—"

In the meantime, urged on by Degas, Mary decided to enter one of her latest paintings in the American section of the international art show at the fair. Degas suggested sending her self-portrait. He thought well of it. He said that except for a certain pensive air it looked much like her, composed and self-contained. He liked the way she had done the flowered bonnet, and the material of her white dress. He liked the diagonal line she made as she half leaned on the arm of the striped sofa. Mary said firmly that she preferred to enter something else, and not put her personal portrait on public display.

All spring she had been working on an unusual and difficult painting—a young girl in a blue armchair. The girl was sprawling, the way small girls do when they plop down and no grownup is present to say, "Sit up straight. Be a lady." The girl was a daughter of a friend of Degas and willing to pose as long as she had Mary's small dog to watch in another blue chair close by.

Degas, dropping in to see how Mary was getting on, was delighted with the way she had done the girl. He said that Mademoiselle obviously had a way with children. Why didn't she paint them more often? She apparently knew just how a child looked and felt.

But she was having trouble with the background, wasn't she? he went on, looking critically at the canvas. With his flair for the unexpected angle, he pulled a third blue chair forward a bit and pushed a small blue sofa back toward the

90

"Little Girl in a Blue Armchair" (*Mary Cassatt*), *1878*

window a little. The result was an interesting arrangement, leaving an oddly shaped empty floor space between the chairs. There, that would be a challenge!

When Mary found that she couldn't make the floor space lie down flat on her canvas, Degas took her brushes briefly and showed her how to achieve the effect she wanted. For the rest, she was on her own.

When the picture was finished, both she and Degas found it so interesting and successful that they agreed that this was the one to enter at the fair.

Again Mary was bitterly disappointed. Her "Little Girl in the Blue Armchair" was rejected. Apparently the jury had balked at the unusual composition. Or did they find the girl's relaxed pose unladylike? Mary felt left out in the cold by her own countrymen. She was indignant, too, because the rejection was, in a way, a slap at Degas. When she discovered that one of the three judges was a pharmacist, she was even more indignant. Pharmacists were useful citizens but they should stick to their pills and pestles and leave art to the experts! She fumed that she would never again have anything to do with juries. Even when they were made up of so-called experts, they were unsatisfactory. Everyone knew that jurymen often traded votes for each other's personal favorites, and how could even the best juror be expected to hold on to any sense of balance or judgment after hours and hours of viewing hundreds and hundreds of paintings? Any juror would develop blind spots and be so stupefied with weariness that he would finally vote a hasty yes or no, just to get the whole thing over with. Mary thought again how right the Impressionists were not to submit their paintings to the whims of official juries. Each artist could best decide for himself what to present to the public. Everybody in the group would just have to work harder to have their own show as soon as possible.

In the following spring, the Impressionists, with renewed courage and a new name, presented their fourth show. Degas insisted they announce themselves as "Independents," although the name never stuck.

Mary was delighted to share in the camaraderie of the artists during the excitement of the hanging and placing of their pictures in rooms on the Avenue de l'Opera, and in the suspense of opening day. One disappointment was that Degas, their headliner, who had promised over thirty works, brought fewer than a dozen. The other Impressionists were annoyed. Mary was, too, but she understood. Degas could not bear to show anything that he considered unfinished or less than perfect.

Just before the opening hour, Mary walked restlessly back and forth from one room to another. It was a wonderful show, she thought. The critics and the public were fools if they too did not think so.

At ten o'clock sharp, the doors were opened to the public. A few people straggled in. They kept coming steadily in two's and three's all day. They were a good-humored lot. There was some laughter; there were some uncomplimentary remarks. But this year there was a subtle change in the atmosphere. People were more receptive. They were trying to understand and accept what they saw.

Mary's most admired painting was one she called simply

"Lydia in a Loge, Wearing a Pearl Necklace" (*Mary Cassatt*),
1879

"La Loge." It was of Lydia, wearing her pearls and a low-cut gown, seated in a box of the curving balcony of the Opéra. The painting stood out because it was in spirit and manner both French and American. The elegant setting was completely French; Lydia looked very American, aglow with the excitement of the evening. She was attractive and had a directness that Mary had caught and presented most effectively. The whole scene shimmered in the light shed by the sparkling chandelier.

The new artist Gauguin, viewing her paintings, said, "Mlle Cassatt has as much charm as Mlle Morisot, but the American has more force." On hearing this, Mary had mixed feelings, because her friend Berthe Morisot Manet was not exhibiting this year. She had other important things to attend to. She was about to have a baby. At any other time Mary might have felt a pang of envy. To be an artist, to be married, and to have your own child to love and to paint—surely a woman couldn't ask for more than that! But today Mary had no time or room for envy. Just to be showing with the Independents, to be one of them, to succeed or to fail with them, was glory enough.

The doors of the exhibit closed at six o'clock. When the admission receipts were counted, the Independents rejoiced together. "We are saved!" That was the word sent to Monet, whose works were there but who had been too afraid of failure to come himself. This was the best opening day they had ever had—nothing spectacular, but encouraging. There was handshaking all around.

And the critics? In the days that followed, Mary and the other artists devoured every word written in the papers.

No critics were lavish in praise, but few were hostile. Degas and Mary Cassatt were singled out for admiring comment by several. George Lafenestre wrote: "M. Degas and Mlle Cassatt are the only artists who distinguish themselves. . . . Both have a lively sense of luminous arrangements in Parisian interiors. . . ."

Another critic, J. K. Huysmans, said ". . . Take a man of great talent like M. Degas, take even his pupil, Miss Mary Cassatt, and see if the works of these artists are not more interesting . . . than all these tinkling little contraptions which hang . . . in the interminable rooms of the exposition."

Happily everyone, including Mary, sold some pictures. And when the final admissions money was counted, that was divided among all the participating artists. With her share Mary promptly bought a Degas and a Monet. Even though Mary regularly exhibited with the Impressionists in later years, she always looked back on that particular exhibition as one of the high points in her career.

In the pleasure she took in all the praise and recognition it brought her, nothing meant more to her than the sight of her father clipping the newspaper notices, writing to his sons Gard and Aleck in America, telling everyone how proud he was of his Mame. Mary was touched, remembering his bewildered opposition so many years before when he had said that he would almost rather see her dead than have his daughter become a professional artist.

CHAPTER XII

Time after time Mary asked herself whether she was in love with Degas. How could she be when so many times she couldn't even stand him? He was the most stimulating, interesting, helpful, and admirable person she had ever known. He was also the most difficult, procrastinating, exasperating, and devastating person she had met in her whole life.

Once he got Mary all involved in doing graphics for a magazine, *Le Jour et la Nuit,* that he planned to publish. She worked day and night for months to learn new skills in different kinds of engraving—line, dry-point, soft ground etching, aquatint. The results were exciting. Then the magazine never saw daylight. Degas dropped it for something else. It was infuriating. But Mary had to admit to herself that his early enthusiasm had helped to launch her on a brand-new and successful phase of her career. Print-making became as rewarding to her as painting. She grew so adept in this art that in later years she won wide recognition. The only drawback was that she found she was putting a great strain on her eyes and had to rest them more frequently.

Mary found that Degas made a charming companion on all sorts of expeditions. When she went to her *modiste* to purchase a new bonnet, he asked to go with her. He sat off to one side, watching and sketching while she tried on various *chapeaux*—flowered hats, feathered hats, hats beribboned and bedecked with all kinds of trimmings. Degas sketched her trying them on before the mirror.

Just as Mary was tempted to think that perhaps, after all, he was looking at her with as much personal as professional interest, he said in a matter-of-fact way that he liked sketching her because she could hold a difficult pose as expertly as a working model.

On the way home, when she queried him, he said, "Do you really want to know why I like to go to the milliner's with you?"

Mary listened eagerly for his answer. He said, "It's because I like to study the young apprentice's red hands as she holds the box of pins for the *modiste*."

"That should teach me!" Mary thought to herself. But the lessons were hard to learn. Just when she decided Degas was impossible and absolutely impervious where she as a woman was concerned, he became tender and attentive. When she was thrown from her horse and badly

Collection of Mrs. Percy C. Madeira, courtesy of the owner.
Photograph by Brenwasser, New York

"Robert Simpson Cassatt on Horseback" (*Mary Cassatt*), 1885

injured, breaking her leg and dislocating a shoulder because her galloping horse stepped into a hole, no one was kinder or more sympathetic than Degas. He wrote her charmingly personal notes, full of tender expressions of his devotion. He brought her bouquets of roses (though he couldn't stand being near flowers).

When she wanted a new dog as a pet, it was Degas who went to endless trouble to get the best sort of Belgian griffon for her. (And he couldn't stand dogs!)

Admiring their friend, the poet Mallarmé, Degas took up the writing of sonnets and dedicated one to Mary. Or, Mary asked herself, was the sonnet really to her pet parrot, Coco? She pondered what meaning lay behind Degas comparing her Coco to Robinson Crusoe's parrot on the remote island? And what meaning lay hidden in the last six lines of the sonnet:

> You are the one who pities him, he does not pity you;
> Your parrot . . . but you should know that like a tiny saint,
> Coco collects his thoughts and goes on reciting
> What your heart told the open-hearted confidant,
> If, besides the tip of his wing, you also clip
> A tip of his tongue, then he is mute . . . and green.

Whatever he might hope it would mean to Mary, it apparently meant something so personal to Degas that he never read it aloud to other people, although he usually could not resist showing off by reading his sonnets for the entertainment of his friends.

Degas kept inviting her to all kinds of artistic events in Paris. They went everywhere together. It was obvious to Mary and to everyone else that he enjoyed her companionship. It occurred to Mary that people might even assume that they were lovers. At the thought, her back just grew straighter. Let them talk! Gossip couldn't touch her!

One year Mary and Degas painted portraits of each other. Before she was finished, Mary decided that perhaps she wasn't very successful in doing men, although she had no trouble in painting her father astride a favorite horse, or her brothers when they came to visit. Now she was so dissatisfied with her attempt to get Degas's complex character down on canvas that she deliberately destroyed the painting. She couldn't bear to have done less than her best or to hear the biting things he would surely have to say about it if he didn't like it.

She was equally dissatisfied, however, with Degas's portrait of her. He made her look—well, ''repugnant'' was the word that came to her mind. It had some artistic merit, but she hoped—in fact, she *knew*—that she did not really look like that blank-faced woman seated leaning forward with her arms on her knees, holding a sheaf of photographs, fanning them out like playing cards. For once Mary bit her tongue, to keep from saying to Degas what she really thought of it. As soon as she could, she put it away. Years later she made sure that it was disposed of by her dealer as a Degas portrait of an unidentified subject. He sold it to someone in Japan.

She liked much better the series that Degas had done of her as she was closely studying a work of art in the Louvre. One of these was a pastel on gray paper, done with great

"A Cup of Tea" (*Mary Cassatt*), *circa 1880*
Lydia Cassatt is at left

style, even wit. No one but Degas could make a back, her back, so eloquent. Everyone admired it.

Then why did he always have to spoil things? This time it was with a typical Degas jibe. He said, ''I wanted to show a woman with crushed respect and absence of all feeling before great works of art.''

Mary was indignant. Crushed respect, indeed! Degas would learn that there was nothing crushed or unfeeling about her! She could be just as independent as he was. He might be a great artist and he might have a way with words, but he was certainly what the French called *mauvais caractère*. At times he was impossible. She would get along better without him for a while.

After all, there were other artists who sought her out. Berthe Morisot Manet, the other woman in the group and now the mother of an enchanting child, Julie, was a good friend, even though she was Mary's rival in the art world. The two women were very different. Where Mary Cassatt was forthright, trim, straight-backed, American, Berthe Morisot was feminine, soft, poetic, French. While never close, the two women respected each other's talents and personalities and enjoyed each other's company.

Berthe and her family gave delightful Thursday-night dinners for some of their good Impressionist friends. Mary went occasionally, enjoying the Manets and their guests. However, Degas was a Thursday-night regular, so if Mary wanted to avoid seeing him, she would have to stay away from the Manets on those evenings.

Mary and her family enjoyed entertaining in their own comfortable apartment. Afternoon tea was a pleasant

daily ceremony, with Mary or her mother presiding behind the heirloom silver tea set for the family and for any
guests who might drop in. Sometimes Mary arranged small
dinner parties. Occasionally the menu featured not only
delectable French dishes but foods sent over from Pennsylvania by the generous Aleck. They were thought very exotic by the French guests: canvasback duck, corn, sweet
potatoes, ham, turkey, cranberry, and sound sweet American apples.

Mary saw to it that good talk sparkled like the good wine
at the table. She thought no artist so stimulating to conversation as Degas. But even when Degas was not there,
she could hold her own talking about art and literature
with other guests like the novelist Zola and the poet Mallarmé. She argued politics vehemently with the up-and-
coming Georges Clemenceau, who, in his early forties, was
considered a Radical leader. Mary admired his collection
of Japanese prints more than she did his politics, but drew
him out on both subjects.

James McNeill Whistler was the most amusing and the
most exasperating of the American artists who visited the
Cassatt apartment. When he came over from his studio in
London, he dressed outrageously and sometimes behaved
outrageously. Mary thought his monocle an absurd affecta-
tion but not so ridiculous as his demand for a medal from
the Salon. When, for his impudence, the jury presented
him with a third-class medal, he was furious. Mary thought
that he deserved it for his vanity but that his paintings
did not. She thought his paintings first-rate and was always ready to put up with his foolishness because both his

art and his conversation were brilliant. She agreed with Degas, who said that Whistler would be the most ridiculous man in Paris if he weren't a genius. And he was a genius.

CHAPTER XIII

Mary's family absorbed much of her time. They could not remember who it was who first amused them by coining the term that described them all—"Cassatturated." In those years, the early eighties, Mary felt that not only she herself but even her work was thoroughly "Cassatturated."

At first she did not have to choose between her work and her family; she happily combined them. They all posed for her—her father in his easy chair or astride his horse, her mother reading aloud to visiting grandchildren, and most of all, her sister Lydia.

When Lydia was still well enough to go out in the Bois in their pony cart, Mary frequently sketched and painted her driving their pony Bichette. The most successful of

"Woman and Child Driving" (Mary Cassatt), 1879
Lydia Cassatt with a niece of Edgar Degas

these paintings showed Lydia, the reins in her hands and a small girl seated at her side. Behind them the youthful groom sat up straight, trying to look grown up and dignified in his tall hat and black coat. Ahead was Bichette, but in this painting only the pony's hind quarters could be seen. This amused the family, who by now were used to Mary's way of sometimes cutting off figures in motion, a way she had learned from Degas.

Mary and Degas saw something of each other again whenever the Impressionists got together. For the painting, "Woman and Child Driving," Mary had even borrowed Degas's sister's child to sit with Lydia. But for a long time Mary had little time for anyone outside her family.

As Lydia grew more and more frail, Mary inwardly seethed that doctors were unable to help. Outwardly she remained calm and bent her energies to painting her sister in quiet home scenes: Lydia working on a piece of tapestry, or holding a cup of tea, knitting in the garden, or just sitting in the sun on the balcony. Mary painted Lydia, not with sentimentality, but with all her skill and with love, as though she were grasping at these last days of companionship with her sister.

Finally Lydia became so ill that she could not pose at all. When she died in the fall of 1882, Mary was desolate. But the whole family were grateful that some of Mary's best work had gone into this lasting record of Lydia's quiet place in their lives.

After Lydia's death, Aleck and his family came to be near the Cassatts in Paris for several months. Although the visitors stayed in a hotel, the whole family saw each other at the apartment every day. The children particularly were a consolation to Mary and her parents. Ed, the first grandchild, was old enough to be put in a French school. But the younger ones, Robbie, Katherine, and little Elsie, were in and out of the apartment all day. They made a cheerful trio.

Their Aunt Mary seized this opportunity to have them pose for her in her studio—sometimes separately, sometimes together.

Mary's interest in print-making was again aroused. She successfully undertook to make dry-point etchings—difficult at any time, but particularly challenging when the models were as lively and energetic as her nieces and nephews.

In dry-point, Mary drew with a "pencil" made of steel directly on a metal plate, usually copper. Of course, once the mark was made, there was no erasing it or changing it, and so it had to be right the first time. It was demanding work and called forth all her skill. Her drawing improved steadily.

When the children grew restless posing, Mary sometimes called in her mother to read to them, or she gave them a picture book to look at, or a toy to handle. Or she herself told them stories. She was firm with them in seeing to it that they stayed still, but her discipline was always fair and good-humored. The children liked her and tried to live up to her expectations.

Aleck had long talks with his parents and with his sister, all of whom depended on him for counsel. The visitors went off on short tours to the South of France and to Italy, but they kept coming back to Paris.

In March, Aleck sat for his portrait. He asked Mary for her advice as to whom he should get to paint his wife Lois, since Mary felt that she would rather not undertake the responsibility of doing Lois herself. Privately, Mary thought that Lois would be hard to please and that it would be better to give someone else the commission.

After thinking it over, Mary recommended Whistler. He was American, he was famous, he was talented, and while he sometimes behaved like a mountebank, he was serious about his painting. No doubt he would do his best to please such an important fellow American as Alexander Cassatt, vice president of the Pennsylvania Railroad.

They were all delighted when Whistler agreed to start the portrait at once if they would come to his London studio. There was a discussion as to what Lois should wear. Aleck, always enthusiastic about horses and riding, urged her to wear her riding habit. Lois was not so sure that this was her most becoming outfit. Even her mother-in-law suggested that no woman looked so well in riding clothes as she did in a formal gown. But Whistler confidently said, "It depends on the painter who does the portrait." He thought the riding habit just right.

And so the sittings began in the artist's Chelsea studio in London. The Cassatts thought Whistler's own garb was very curious; he wore an American bartender's white jacket. But he was polite, he did not behave like a wild eccentric, and he concentrated on trying to create a fine portrait. There was just one difficulty. By the end of the month, when the agreed-upon time was up and the agreed-upon sum was paid and the Aleck Cassatts had to sail for home, the portrait was not finished. Whistler promised to finish it right away and to send it after them. But days, weeks, the summer went by. Still no portrait.

Mary felt as frustrated as Aleck. She understood better than he could an artist's reluctance to call anything finished. Still, this was outrageous; Whistler wasn't even trying to finish it. Mary's father took to muttering about "that miserable fellow." Mary suggested that if Whistler did not soon deliver the promised painting, she herself would try to confront Whistler when she was in London on vacation with her mother.

CHAPTER XIV

How Mary wished that there were no Channel between France and England; crossing it was always torture for her. In August of '83 Mary took her mother on holiday, first for a stay in Cowes, a resort on the Isle of Wight; then on to London for a short visit and to see Whistler. Mary could ride a horse superbly and could walk for miles without tiring, but she became seasick as soon as she set foot on the heaving deck of a Channel vessel. At the end of the passage she had to be carried off the boat.

It took Mary days to recover enough to begin to enjoy the festivities in Cowes and to stop shuddering at the sight of the yachts bobbing up and down in the harbor. Gard, her brother, was a yachting enthusiast. He and his bride, Jennie, joined the Cassatts there for a while, adding to their enjoyment of the place, though Gard could never persuade Mary to go out on the water with them.

When Mary and her mother went on to London, Mary was afraid that the city would be dreadfully dull because the fine-art galleries were all closed in August. How she wished she could have been there earlier when in the spring Durand-Ruel, the faithful friend and dealer, had presented the first London exhibition of Impressionist paintings including two of her own. But at that time she had been too busy with family visitors to leave home.

Now in London they were hospitably received by two of their favorite cousins from America who were staying in one of the best hotels and who insisted that the Cassatts be their guests. Mrs. Riddle and her daughter, Annie Scott, were good companions as they all went on excursions and various drives together.

One of the first things Mary did was to arrange to go to Whistler's to insist that he finish Lois's portrait at once. Whistler was not there. Was he avoiding her? Mary was sure of it. He had left word with a pupil to admit her and to show her his studio. There she saw the portrait of Lois, standing tall in her riding habit, riding crop in hand. Mary thought it a fine portrait, but it was definitely not finished and there was no sign that Whistler was working on it. All Mary could do was to leave urgent word for the artist to finish it at once and send it to her brother as promised.

She had a feeling that her message wouldn't do a bit of good. Whistler was too much like the butterfly that he often used as his signature—flitting about, difficult to catch, and hard to pin down. As it turned out, it was two years before Aleck got the finished portrait.

But now Mary settled down to enjoying the London shops. First she bought wedding presents for Gard and Jennie, and for her old friend Louisine Elder, who was being married that very month to Henry O. Havemeyer, a most successful businessman in New York. Mary bought some fine tweeds for herself and admired magnificent displays of English silver and chinaware. She searched for interesting jewelry in antique shops, being particularly fond of curious old finger rings.

Once she stopped short in front of a window, attracted by a lovely old Japanese tea and coffee set. The deep blue of the porcelain caught her eye. The handsome shape of the teapot, the round cups without handles, set in their deep saucers, the interesting designs of all the pieces, including the containers for sugar and cream—all these delighted her. She longed for it. But Mary decided she could not afford the set; it would be sheer self-indulgence to buy it. But what marvelous color and design had gone into the making of it. It was a work of art!

Soon after Mary and her mother returned to Paris, an enormous package arrived from England. In it was the coveted tea set, sent by the cousin, Annie Scott. Already overwhelmed by the generous hospitality of her cousins while she was in London, Mary now wondered how she could ever repay them. They were coming over to Paris soon to stay at a nearby hotel. Why not paint a portrait of Mrs. Riddle and present it to her daughter? That would be something unique, something they could not buy for themselves in any shop.

The ladies were charmed with the proposal. And so the sittings began. Mary had the happy idea of posing Mrs.

Riddle behind the tea table, which was set with several glowing pieces of the newly acquired Japanese tea set. The lady, dignified, gracious, was shown as obviously accustomed to the role of hostess, but Mary wanted to make the painting much more than that of a well-bred lady serving tea. She threw herself into making it a great painting of strong design and interesting composition. In addition, she took particular care to make what she hoped was a convincing likeness of the sitter. She was anxious to have Annie Scott approve the way she did her mother's face—her blue eyes, her beautiful, rather large nose, her gentle mouth—for she knew that a likeness would be more important to the cousins than any other artistic elements of the painting.

When the canvas was finished, her own family thought it a good likeness, but Mary knew it would be better not to show it to the cousins themselves until it was handsomely framed. That made such a difference to people who were not artists. Though Mary herself thought the portrait one of the best things she had done, in her anxiety she called in Degas. He would tell her exactly what he thought of it. To her relief and delight, Degas said positively that the portrait was ''distinction itself.''

Finally the painting, in a handsome Louis XVI gold frame, was shown to Mrs. Riddle and Annie Scott. It was put on the easel, displayed in the best light. The ladies murmured pleasant things about it. Mary had done the tea set so well! And the material in the dress was beautifully done. The lace in the cap was almost real. As to the face, well—they hesitated: the eyes were perfect, so blue.

"Lady at the Tea Table" (*Mary Cassatt*), *1883–85*

And the mouth was just right. But the nose! There was something about the nose. Wasn't it a bit large? Wasn't it in fact much too large? Somehow it spoiled the rest, so that the portrait really didn't at all flatter the subject, did it? Perhaps Cousin Mary could change the nose somehow?

Mary was so taken aback at this reaction that she in turn murmured something vague about seeing what she could do. After the ladies had departed, she gazed a long while at the painting. She agreed with Degas. But to the dear cousins for whom it was intended as a thank-you present, it was a total failure. She simply couldn't work any more on it—not now, at any rate. Mary quickly put the portrait in a closet and firmly shut the door.

CHAPTER XV

During the rest of the 1880's Mary Cassatt frequently had to choose between her family and her painting. Often it was her family who needed all her time and attention. Her mother's rheumatism and heart trouble worsened, alarming Mary. She developed a bad cough, too. She had to stay indoors most of the time because the doctor said that the five flights of stairs were too much for her. If only they had an elevator!

Mary began spending much of each day looking for a suitable apartment with a lift. Mr. Cassatt refused to help; he dreaded any move, thought any change unnecessary, balked at the very thought of being uprooted from their familiar and comfortable surroundings. He could climb any number of flights of stairs without losing breath, he walked six miles a day; he didn't see why his womenfolk couldn't do the same. Wasn't Mary exaggerating the need for a move? Why not take her mother where it was warm and sunny, away from the gray Paris winter? Mary could leave the apartment problem until later. He would stay and look after things at home.

And so Mary undertook an expedition to Spain, organizing her forces like a field marshal. Mathilde, the long-time companion and housekeeper, helped with the packing of trunks and boxes and bags. Mary optimistically packed her own painting equipment. It was she who bought the tickets for the long train trip, who found a porter at the station, first boarded the train, found a compartment which they could keep to themselves and into which they could all fit, helped Mathilde assist the invalid into the compartment, and supervised the porter stowing away the dozen travel cases, the medicine kit, the shawls, the packets of books and newspapers, the afternoon tea basket—all the time holding firmly under one arm Battie, the dog, who wriggled with excitement and pleasure at setting off on such an adventure.

In Spain, Mary's mother did seem to improve somewhat; at least her cough disappeared. But her rheumatism bothered her and she developed devastating headaches, so that Mary had to turn to a Spanish doctor for help. In desperation, she wrote, too, to Aleck, urging that he write his father, making him understand that they must move to an apartment house where there was an elevator before her mother's return to Paris. "Maybe he will listen to you," Mary wrote. "He won't listen to me."

Mr. Cassatt did listen to his son and finally gave his consent to a move, but he said Mary must look for the apartment herself since she was the one who insisted upon the change. Her father washed his hands of the whole problem.

By now Mrs. Cassatt was better, and Mary shepherded her little flock to Biarritz for the rest of the winter because her mother felt more at home in France than in Spain. And her cousins, Mrs. Riddle and Annie Scott, were in Biarritz for the season. Fortunately, the matter of Mrs. Riddle's portrait was tactfully forgotten by the ladies.

Soon Mary decided she could leave her mother to Mathilde's devoted if not very skillful nursing and the companionship of the cousins while she returned to Paris to go apartment hunting again. After weeks of looking, she found a comfortable, not too expensive, apartment at 14, rue Pierre-Charron. The building was in a pleasant, rather fashionable neighborhood, though far from shops and tradesmen. To Mary the two best things about it were the elevator for her mother and an extra room which she could use as a studio, so that when she could finally get back to her painting she would no longer have to keep up a separate studio.

Her painting? How she longed to get back to work! There was no time, no energy left for that now. There was the moving to supervise, her father to soothe and to settle in the new place, and then the trip back to Biarritz to bring her mother home. This was one of those years when Mary had to choose between her family and her painting. When they needed her, there was nothing to do but choose her family.

In the summer, Mary was glad to get back to her easel. First she found a villa to rent outside of Paris where the country-loving Cassatts could stay for a few months, enjoying relaxed outdoor life. Mrs. Cassatt could sometimes leave her wheelchair to walk out to the carriage or enjoy a short stroll in the garden. Mary's father sometimes found the country dull with few men to talk to except the gardener and the groom, though he always enjoyed riding his horse.

Mary frequently painted out of doors, although she was always more interested in figures than in landscape. A small garden, a lattice, a bit of greenery made a pleasing background for figures. For Mary a wide landscape was to take walks in, to ride in—not to paint. In the late afternoon she would mount her horse and go for a brisk ride, galloping away her fatigue and the cramp in her muscles from long periods of standing or sitting still at her work.

In the fall, Mary always felt the pull of Paris. When the air grew brisk and the pulse of the city quickened, her pulse quickened, too, as she rejoined the heady art world. After a period of separation, she and Degas were always eager to see each other and appraise each other's summer work.

CHAPTER XVI

Degas had been right in urging the Impressionists to call themselves Independents. Members of the original group had gone off in different directions and had become very independent indeed.

In the winter of 1885 and the spring of 1886 there was much talk, argument, hope, and controversy among them as to whether they should try to have a group showing. There had been none since 1882, and even then Degas had refused to exhibit because a friend of his, Raffaelli, was not invited to show. Mary, always loyal to Degas in matters of art, had also declined to show.

Now, when the Impressionists tried to reorganize for an exhibit, some of them refused unless they could bring in certain outsiders. Degas wanted to include a few newcomers like Vicomte Lepic, who, being more conventional, would help the group win public approval. Pissarro argued for the admission of two new young artists, Paul Signac and Georges Seurat, who had adopted an entirely new method of painting. They put a myriad of tiny dots of different colors side by side, counting on the spectator, standing a certain distance away from the painting, to mix the colors with his own eye. Pissarro insisted that Seurat in particular was a ''scientific impressionist,'' as opposed to the ''romantic impressionists,'' who he maintained were becoming old-fashioned.

Berthe Morisot's husband, Eugène Manet, who was trying to help organize the show, was violently opposed to Seurat's being admitted. Degas's only objection was that Seurat's painting, ''A Sunday Afternoon on La Grande Jatte'' was so big that it would cover an entire wall. On the other hand, he objected to the inclusion of Gauguin, with whom he had quarreled. Monet and Renoir decided that they would stay out of the whole thing and show instead at Petit's Exposition Internationale.

Some of the original members, remembering how Degas always promised much and delivered little, wanted to keep him in the background. Degas, never one to stay in the background of any venture, had much to say about how the show should be run. He insisted that their show should take place at the same time as the official Salon, as another gesture of rivalry with the Salon and of confidence in themselves. Mary Cassatt agreed.

Pissarro said, ''It doesn't matter to Degas and Miss Cassatt whether they sell or not. But it does matter to those of us who wonder where our next meal is coming from.''

Mary's only insistence was that, if she helped finance the show, her name must not be publicized. She had always objected, as did Berthe Morisot, to having her name on posters or listed in advertisements. Ladies did not have their names plastered all over Paris like actresses. Besides, Mary felt that her work should speak for itself and that her name should appear only in her signature on her canvases.

After all the arguments and all the disputes were settled, compromises made, some people left out, others allowed in, the eighth and last show of the Impressionsts as a group opened on May 15, 1886, over the Restaurant Dorée at 1, rue Lafitte, the street of art dealers and art shops.

Mary Cassatt, Degas, and Berthe Morisot Manet put up the money for the rent. They expected little or no financial return from the show, but wanted to give their group one more chance to show what they were doing. They purposely left out of all announcements the words ''Impressionist,'' and ''Independents,'' calling the showing simply ''Eighth Exhibition of Paintings.''

Degas entered two of his pastels called ''At the Milliner's.'' Mary had posed for them but of course was not named by Degas as the model. They were not meant to be portraits. His other important entries were seven in a series of nudes, of ''Women bathing, washing, drying, rubbing down, combing their hair or having it combed.'' Degas felt it was an important departure in art for him to show nudes, not self-consciously posed for an audience or even

"At the Milliner's" (*Edgar Degas*)

the artist, but caught in natural attitudes as they were when nobody was watching.

One spectator said he felt as though he were looking at them through a keyhole. It was inevitable that some of the public thought the pictures obscene. Mary stoutly defended them as highest art.

Her own most talked-of oil was called "Girl Arranging Her Hair." The painting was of a red-headed adolescent, not at all pretty—rather homely, in fact—with mouth open, showing prominent teeth, and twisting her hair with upraised arm as she looked in her mirror. The public's usual response to this was "What an ugly duckling"!

This painting was the direct result of a challenge on the part of Degas, who scoffed that no woman painter, not even Mary, knew what style was; not style in the sense of fashion, of course, but style in art, in drawing. Mary painted this picture to prove him wrong. When he saw it, Degas said at once, "What drawing! What style! I must have it for my own collection."

Berthe Morisot had a number of paintings in the exhibition, as did most of the others. The sensation of the show, however, was Seurat's "La Grande Jatte," made up of thousands of dots of color, covering an enormous canvas that dominated one whole room. It showed people on a sunny Sunday afternoon relaxing on the green grass of an island in the Seine. Everyone looked absolutely still, frozen in his pose as though under an enchantment. There were ladies with their smoothly rounded bustles, holding round parasols; gentlemen in top hats and with walking sticks; children caught suspended skipping in mid-air; dogs snif-

133

fing the grass; and, most entertaining of all, a lady's pet monkey on a leash, his tail curling upward in a long loop. Everything was stylized, everything was pattern. Seurat had taken an Impressionist's sunny scene and made it his own, putting it together with a million dots of color and peopling it with paper dolls. It was original, it was charming, it was amusing, and it was disturbing—disturbing not only to the public, who had to back away from it in order to see it, but to the critics, one of whom referred to the dots as "colored fleas." Its new technique was disturbing to the older Impressionists as well, to all except Pissarro, who for a while painted that way himself.

Disapproval of this painting and of the artist Seurat was one of the reasons Monet and Renoir would not take part in this show but instead exhibited in Petit's successful Exhibition Internationale. Georges Petit, a dealer formerly with Durand-Ruel, had left to set up his own rival shop. When Monet and Renoir deserted their old dealer and let Petit handle some of their work, they said that they did it in order to show the public that more than one dealer believed in them. Their departure was a terrific blow to Durand-Ruel, who was already having financial troubles. Indeed, his situation had been so desperate that Mary Cassatt lent him money so that he would not have to close his shop. She was indirectly responsible, too, for help that came from America. He was invited by the American Art Association to show his Impressionist paintings in the United States.

Since at the time most of Mary's paintings were in the group show in Paris, Durand-Ruel, arriving in the States,

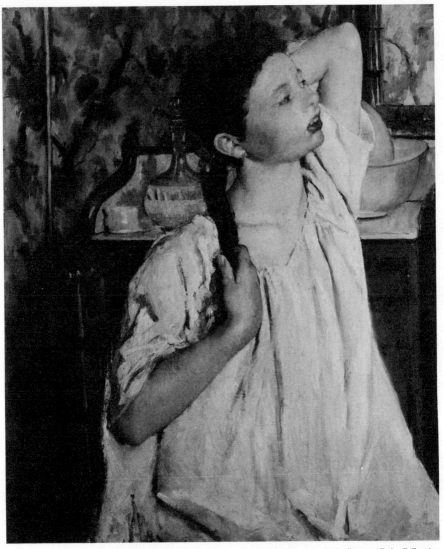

"Girl Arranging Her Hair" (*Mary Cassatt*), *1886*

had to borrow from Aleck a few of Mary's paintings, including one of her mother, "Portrait of a Lady," and "Family Group," the one of her mother reading to Aleck's children. Lousine Elder Havemeyer also lent some of her paintings.

With intense interest Mary followed the uncertain fortunes of Durand-Ruel's show in New York, a collection of three hundred paintings which he called "Works in Oil and Pastel by the Impressionists of Paris." New York proved friendly and responsive to the paintings, Mary having helped pave the way to understanding by having already interested American collectors in the Impressionists. The success of this history-making show led Durand-Ruel later to set up a branch gallery in New York.

Mary realized, however, that she was still a long way from the recognition in her own country that she was winning in France. And even in France, as the Impressionists scattered after their last show in Paris, Mary knew that sooner or later she would have to make it on her own.

CHAPTER XVII

In 1890 a vast Japanese Exhibition at the Beaux Arts set all of Paris agog. Degas invited Mary to go see it with him. He wanted to share this latest eye-opening experience with her. However much they argued with each other, they would rather go to exhibits together than with anyone else.

For some time, artists had been interested in the pieces of Oriental art that found their way to the Western world. One of Mary's prized possessions was her blue antique tea and coffee set given her by Mrs. Riddle. Even the politician Clemenceau was an enthusiastic collector of Japanese art. As for Whistler, he liked to pick up prints and porcelains, fans and costumes, whenever he could to put in his paintings.

Now here gathered together for the first time in one place was a huge display of almost a thousand Japanese prints, hundreds of books containing woodcuts, pieces of porcelain, and Japanese screens.

Mary, like Degas, was exhilarated by the exciting display, particularly of the prints. She responded eagerly to this kind of Japanese art—its strangeness, its simplicity, flatness, lack of shadow, its color, its pattern. She collected Japanese prints so that she could study them at home. She began to do things in the Japanese manner. In the past she had done dry-points in order constantly to improve her drawing. Now, stimulated by Japanese prints, she undertook a whole series of color prints. While she tried for some of the Oriental effects, her own method of gaining these effects was different and very much her own.

She drew outlines on copper plates in dry-points, then laid on a soft ground in those parts she wanted to color. She twisted small rags over small pointed sticks, dipped them in color, and applied them in different areas on each of three plates so that the colors would not run together. She then had a printer help her. Together they ran the heavy plates through a hand press, something like a mangle. It was hard work; sometimes they worked eight hours a day in order to get their proofs.

It was more than worth the effort, for the final results were stunning. Among her prints was one she called "The Toilette." It showed the back of a woman, bare to the waist, leaning over a basin of water on a washstand. The Japanese influence could be seen in many aspects of the print, including the angle, the woman's striped skirt, the patterned rug, and the flowered pitcher. But the basic drawing was superb, and that was Mary's own.

When she showed the finished print to Degas, he was greatly impressed and was extravagant in his praise. Mary, who had braced herself for criticism, let down her guard. Whereupon, as though he regretted having said so much, Degas said, "I will not admit that a woman can draw so well."

Mary wondered if she would ever learn! There was a barb hidden in every compliment of Degas's, as though he were afraid to show his real feelings. She knew that she was not the only one who felt crushed by his devastating remarks. Moreau, a painter and good friend, got to the point where he could no longer take Degas's biting comments. He said that if he were going to accomplish anything and lead his own life, he would have to stop seeing Degas. Mary often felt the same way. She had been proud to be his disciple and to belong to the Impressionist group which he had helped organize, but now it looked as though the group in Paris were rapidly dissolving.

When in 1891 a few of the Impressionists, with more outsiders, organized a new group, the Société des Peintres-Graveurs Français, Mary assumed that she would be asked to join. But there was an unexpected catch. While Mary was recognized as both a painter and an engraver, she was, after all, not really French. Being foreign-born, she was barred from membership in the new group.

Though Mary knew that the rule was not a slight to her personally, she felt snubbed nonetheless. Very well! If the new group did not need her, she did not need them. She

"The Toilette" (Mary Cassatt), 1891

could go it alone, and she would do just that. She would arrange to have her own one-man show at Durand-Ruel's. This could well be the right time to take that daring plunge!

Mary found that Pissarro, too, was indignant. He had exhibited in every Impressionist show from the beginning, yet he was banished from the new Society because he had been born in the British West Indies. He tugged furiously at his white beard and railed against the new group, whom he began disdainfully to call the "Patriots" because they were trying to make art a matter of citizenship and birth certificates.

Pissaro was glad to join Mary in her rebellion. After months of planning and work, each put on a one-man show at the same place and the same time in the spring that the new Society was exhibiting. The large group of "Patriots" had the big gallery at Durand-Ruel's. Mary and Pissaro each had a little room adjoining the gallery.

Mary's was a small showing, but choice: there were a few oils and pastels and ten or twelve of her marvelous color prints. Pissarro was as enthusiastic about her entries as he was about his own. He wrote to his son, Lucien, an artist in London, that Mlle Cassatt's colored engravings were rare and exquisite and that the "Patriots" would be furious when they realized how "ugly, heavy, and lusterless" their own engravings would seem by contrast.

Whether they were furious or not, they were certainly annoyed by Mary's audacity in setting up her own rival show next door. Degas praised her prints, but the other artists were noncommittal.

However, through Degas, Mary was invited to a dinner in honor of the Society's official opening, given at the home of a sculptor-painter friend of Degas's, Paul-Albert Bartholomé. To show that she bore them no ill will, Mary attended, but she was soon sorry that she had. The members began to tease her about her brashness in setting up her own exhibit. At the beginning of the evening she accepted this with good humor, giving them *tac au tac,* or tit for tat, but when they persisted in badgering her about her defiant independence and would not let the subject drop, she became annoyed and then upset.

Mary had worked hard for months on her prints and to get a small but impressive show together. Worn out from days and nights of preparation and from the strain of hanging her pictures, she was anxious about the reaction of critics and of the public. She was astonished at the reaction of these fellow artists who were taking it all so personally. Were they envious, as Pissarro thought? Men were just as petty and jealous as women, Mary decided—perhaps more so!

Even Degas, who had praised her work, did not spare her his sarcastic witticisms about women. Finally she became so upset that angry tears stung her eyes and she left the party abruptly. She was not going to put up with this another minute. And she was determined that none of them should see her cry—certainly not Degas!

Mary soon recovered from the annoyance of that particular evening and enjoyed the mild success that her own small exhibit began to have. This spurred her to take the plunge two years later into another independent showing.

This one was much more ambitious, much larger, presenting almost a hundred prints, pastels, and paintings. Altogether her work was so impressive that it convinced everyone that she was not dependent on any group. Mary Cassatt was an artist in her own right. Her work was acclaimed by critics, by friends, by the public, and even by the "Patriots." It had taken a long time, but now, nearing the age of fifty, Mary Cassatt the American had made her own place in the art world of France.

But in America? So far, she had made little impression on her native land.

CHAPTER XVIII

Whether or not Mary Cassatt was well known at home, she wanted passionately to have some of the best of art, old and new, hung in the museums there where young Americans could grow up in its splendor. She felt strongly that new generations ought not to have to cross the ocean as she had in order to study the finest. Mary worked with all the zeal of a missionary to persuade American friends to build up private collections, with the hope that some day these would be given to museums in the States.

The most avid collectors among her friends were the Havemeyers of New York. Just as the young Louisine Elder had followed Mary's lead in appreciating and buying her first Degas, her first Whistler, her first Impressionists, so now on their trips to Paris Louisine Havemeyer and her husband turned to Mary for guidance. They had unlimited funds, highly developed taste, and an insatiable appetite for tracking down the best in art for their magnificent home gallery. They proudly bought several fine Cassatts, which pleased Mary, of course. But it pleased her just as much to take the Havemeyers to the studios and galleries of Paris, where they saw and bought glowing Manets, Monets, paintings by Degas, and other notable examples of Impressionism.

Beside the Havemeyers and her own brother, Aleck, there were others who turned to Mary for advice about art purchases—people like the Whittemores, the Sears family, and James Stillman, the wealthy American banker.

Separated from his wife, Mr. Stillman lived in Paris in lonely splendor. He admired Mary Cassatt, perhaps was even in love with her. He was drawn by her magnetic personality, her lively conversation. He liked the way she carried herself, the crisp stylish way she dressed. He even enjoyed the way she talked back when he mildly disagreed with her over anything from the choice of a wine to the purchase of a painting.

Mary would not let him buy any painting that she thought sweet or sentimental, such as an inferior one by the artist Greuze that he thought he wanted. Instead she led him to appreciate and buy old masters like Rembrandt. Once in the gallery of Gimpel, an art dealer, she tried to persuade him to buy a fine Velázquez. In the end she said impatiently, "You must buy this canvas; it's shameful to be rich like you. Such a purchase will redeem you." Stillman just smiled as he took out his checkbook.

He admired Mary's own works and without any suggestion from her bought many of them. She did insist that he buy other Impressionists as well. It was really Mary who made a collector of him.

Then she made another convert, the rich and charming social leader from Chicago, Mrs. Potter Palmer. When these two spirited ladies met over the tea table in Paris, Mary recalled in vivid detail how they had almost met eighteen years earlier but were prevented from doing so by nothing less than the great Chicago fire.

Mrs. Palmer took to Mary at once. They both had America and France in their blood; each appreciated the best that each country had to offer. On Mary's advice, Mrs. Palmer bought her first Degas. Paintings by Monet and Renoir also were taken back and hung on the marble and brocaded walls of the Palmer castle—the first Impressionist works to be seen in the Middle West. Eventually some of these would be in the Chicago Art Institute, where all could enjoy them.

Mary always pushed the work of others, never her own, but Mrs. Palmer was so impressed by her paintings and prints that in 1891 she asked Mary to do murals for a section of the Women's Building of the Columbia Exposition to be held in Chicago in 1893. Of course, her choice of Miss Cassatt would have to be approved by her Board of Lady Managers of the Exposition, but she smilingly ventured to guess that there would be little difficulty in persuading them. Mary could see that Mrs. Palmer was a very persuasive lady.

Before anything was settled, Mary and her mother were

shocked when Mary's father died in early December of
1891. He had always been so ready to listen to her about
her work, so much a part of her life, that Mary could not
believe he would never again sit in his favorite chair, looking over his glasses as he advised her what to do or told
her what he himself refused to do.

She was glad that he had not been stubborn when, a few
years before, it had become necessary to make another
move to the new and more conveniently located apartment
at 10, rue de Marignan. He had liked living here near the
Champs-Elysées. Mary was glad, too, that he had seen and
been proud of her first little one-man show the previous
spring. And how delighted he had been when Gard's wife,
Jennie, and little Gardner came over to spend this Christmas with them! Well, it would be a sad Christmas without
her father.

When her father died, Mary cabled her brothers at
once, but it was another week before she felt able to sit
down to write. At last, on black-bordered paper, she wrote
a letter to Aleck and Gard, telling them the details, and
saying what a comfort it was to have Jennie and Gard's
small son with them. Little Gardner had gone into his
grandfather's room and seeing him so quiet had said,
"Poor Grandfather has a bad headache."

Mary said they would all go south for a while. "I think
it will do Mother good; I am very much depressed in every
way and long for a change." She and her mother spent the
rest of the winter in Antibes in the good sun of the Medi-
terranean. They rented a villa very close to the beautiful
Hôtel du Cap d'Antibes. Jennie and little Gardner, who

stayed with them for a while, helped to soften their sadness. They enjoyed walking in the nearby green park among the flower beds and along the sea, sometimes diverted by the sight of the Russian grand dukes and duchesses who came and went from the elegant hotel and who disported themselves in the sea and in the gardens.

Mary did little work but enjoyed sketching and painting her young nephew. She began thinking about the murals for Chicago that she hoped she would be commissioned to do. It would be a tremendous undertaking and different from anything she had ever tried before. She was eager to get started.

CHAPTER XIX

When the persuasive Mrs. Palmer convinced her ladies'
committee that Miss Cassatt was America's finest woman
painter, Mary was told to go ahead with the murals. It was
summertime. She and her mother had gone back to Paris
and left again for the country, to a modest château that
they had rented before, where there were acres of ground
and enough room to paint the murals out-of-doors. Mary
plunged into the tremendous job with all her energies and
skill.

She knew that at the Exposition in Chicago her pictures
would be raised to an immense height, so the figures would
have to be at least life-size in order to be seen at all. She
had never before attempted anything so big.

Her first step was to have a glass-roofed structure built

to protect her work from the weather. Then she had a deep ditch dug in which to lower the mural so that she could paint the upper portion freely without having to climb and perch on a high ladder. Her theme was to be "Young Women Plucking the Fruits of Knowledge and Science." In spite of the allegorical title, Mary certainly did not intend to turn her women into ancient Greek goddesses. She dressed her modern models in modern fashions and showed them picking real fruit in a real orchard.

Mary worked early and late all summer and autumn. Before she finished, she longed to ask Degas to come and give his opinion, but she dared not risk it. He hated coming to the country. If he came, Mary would have to shut up her dogs because he disliked them, and when he ventured out doors he had to wear large dark glasses to protect his eyes and he held a kerchief to his nose so he wouldn't smell the flowers. She knew that if Degas came now and were in a bad mood, he would upset her. She suspected that he might think her murals too simple, too decorative, and lacking the force she showed in her smaller, more intimate work. If he urged her to make any changes, she would never be able to get the pictures to Chicago in time for the opening. At least Durand-Ruel, who saw them, thought they were good and even wished he could buy them.

More important, Mrs. Palmer and her Board liked the murals and had them put in place in the Woman's Building, but they were so high that visitors had to crane their necks in order to see them at all. Mary felt that her pictures could make very little impact on anyone. When she

Detail from the center of Mary Cassatt's mural, "Modern Woman," in the Woman's Building, World's Columbian Exposition of 1893, Chicago

heard after the Exposition that the building had been demolished and with it her murals, she felt sad, remembering that other time long ago when her early paintings were swallowed up by the great fire in that same city. Even though her murals did not seem to have been much of a success, Mary was glad that the Columbian Exposition had apparently done much to arouse her countrymen's interest in art of all kinds.

Meanwhile, Mary had fallen so much in love with a château near Beauvais outside the village of Mesnil-Theribus that she decided to buy it. What bliss it would be to have her own summer place instead of always renting from unpredictable landlords those unpredictable country houses with their all too predictable ancient plumbing! What bliss it would be to own this lovely house with its quiet pond and magnificent trees. And what bliss it was finally to buy and pay for the château with her own money made from her own paintings!

The house needed much repair work and restoration, but in 1893 things were far enough along so that Mary and her mother could happily move in. There was still much landscaping and gardening to be done, but Mary said she looked forward to that, "to making pictures of living things."

The house, a large seventeenth-century hunting lodge, was a picture itself, set back from the road across a sweep of green lawn and framed by great trees. The fine ash trees that must have given the place its name, "Beaufresne," had long since disappeared, but magnificent chestnuts and poplars still stood and had been there as long as anyone could remember. An interesting hexagonal bell tower on each end of the house gave it dignity. The château was not overwhelmingly grand; its charm for Mary lay in its harmonious lines, in the subtle coloring of the rosy-red bricks, and above all in its livability.

Inside, she enjoyed the many rooms with their high ceilings and long, shuttered windows—particularly the graceful oval drawing room. She had her own painting room at the end of the house and delighted, too, in the long, glassed-in sun room that ran along the garden side of the house. Here on the inner wall she put up many of her Japanese prints. The walls of every room began to glow with her collection of Impressionist paintings. These were always more important to her in making a house attractive than were the comfortable furnishings.

When the last painting, the last Degas drawing was in place, Mary looked around her with satisfaction. At last she had her own home where she could care for her ailing mother and where she could welcome her visiting brothers and their families. There would be room enough for them all under one roof.

Mary Cassatt with Madame Joseph Durand-Ruel at Beaufresne

CHAPTER XX

In the nineties, Mary was drawn more and more to painting mothers and children. When anyone asked "Why?" Mary countered with "Why not?" Children made surprisingly good models. Even when they wriggled like tadpoles, they were an interesting challenge to her. She knew children and liked them. They liked her because there was no nonsense about her; they knew where they stood with her.

Her small nieces and nephews, Aleck's and Gard's children, loved to visit her in the country. There they could devour quantities of strawberries grown on the place, feed the ducks in the pond, and ride in the rowboat. They tagged around after the gardener as he took care of the thousand rosebushes their aunt had him plant, and went fishing with him to catch the fat trout that tasted somewhat muddy but somehow delicious when sautéed by the cook in the large, busy kitchen.

There was always the parrot, Coco, to talk to and to tease; the small, nipping dogs to play with; a pony to ride; and a couple of goats to be wary of. Even when a child fell into the pond, as Ellen Mary, Gard's small daughter, did in the first five minutes of her visit and had to be fished out sopping wet, children thought the place a paradise. Sometimes their aunt would drive them into the village. Once, to their delight, she bought them wooden shoes from the old cobbler. The boys clumped around in them with pride and discomfort.

In between hours of play they took turns sitting for their portraits. Sometimes they found it tiresome sitting still so long, but Aunt Mary had toys and books in her studio for them. Once, when two small nieces were restless while posing, Mary called in their mother and had her read *Huckleberry Finn* aloud to them. They all got to laughing so hard—even Mary—that they had to stop the sitting for that morning.

To Mary there was something even more basic than just the personal satisfaction of doing likenesses of her brother's children. When they weren't on hand, she brought in mothers from the neighborhood, who were glad to stop their chores for "notre mademoiselle," as they called her, who paid them for just sitting or standing with their children in their arms. Sometimes it turned out to be harder work than they thought. But Mary liked to do these mothers who never had a nursemaid for their children, because

160

"Gardner and Ellen Mary Cassatt"
Mary Cassatt's portrait of her nephew and niece, done during her
visit to America in 1899

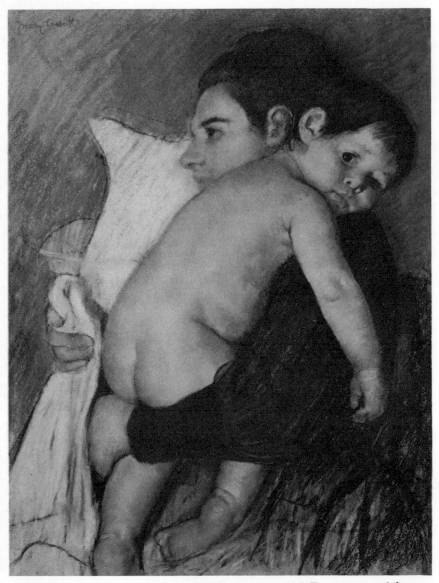

"Maternity, with Baby Observing Spectator" (Mary Cassatt), circa 1890

they relaxed into interesting and natural poses: holding their infants, dressing them, giving them a sponge bath, washing and drying them, bending over them, clasping a small hand or foot.

Mary didn't have sentimental notions about maternity, but she vividly remembered Correggio's joyous infants in the dome of the San Paolo in Parma, naked and unself-conscious in their amusing attitudes. Surely, she thought, a modern woman painter could, as well as a man, understand and capture the unself-conscious gestures of a modern child.

Mary's close relationship with her own mother grew even closer and more tender as Mrs. Cassatt became ill and helpless. Mary willingly gave up her painting in order to sit by her mother's bed hour after hour, until she died in October 1895. Now Mary felt very much alone, with none of her family left in France, and she counted more and more on her brothers' visits and on friends like the Havemeyers.

Back in Paris after summers in the country, Mary often saw Degas and counted as always on his criticism of her work. He was pleased with her paintings of mothers and children. He had always urged that the childhood theme was properly that of a woman painter. But sometimes Degas teased her about always painting rosy, clean, healthy children. "That is the kind I know and see," Mary said reasonably. "Do you want me to make a point of looking for children who are ragged and dirty like the slum children Whistler paints?"

Mary reminded Degas that he had always said that artists should paint the people they see in their everyday world. "These are the children I see, and baths are part of their everyday world." She added, "You yourself are always painting women bathing, showing them stepping in and out of their tubs, washing and stretching and drying themselves like cats."

Degas remarked wryly that he was afraid the bath was a part of the daily life of his models only when they were in his studio, stepping in and out of his tin tub.

Nevertheless, he was impressed by many of Mary's mother-and-child pictures, particularly "The Bath," showing a mother holding her daughter in her lap and washing her feet. He admired Mary's handsome adaptation of Japanese ideas of pattern and color and the addition of her own forceful feeling for structure. There was a sturdy natural look about the mother and child which did not hide the innate tenderness of the scene.

Degas still took Mary to various events in Paris, but it was never very long before he said something she found insulting, or they quarreled over something they cared passionately about, either in art or in politics. When that happened, neither gave in an inch. Then it would take a long separation and long remorseful letters to make peace between them.

One time, back in Paris after another summer at the château, Mary brought to Durand-Ruel's shop a painting she called "Boy Before the Mirror." Degas, dropping into the gallery later, was bowled over by it. "It's the picture of the century," he cried. "Where is Mademoiselle? I must find her at once to congratulate her."

"The Bath" (Mary Cassatt), 1892

In his enthusiasm, Degas had completely forgotten that the last time he and Mary Cassatt had been together they had parted abruptly after one of their heated arguments. Now they were glad to meet again. Mary listened to his perceptive comments about every detail of the picture. After all, Degas's opinion still meant more to her than anyone else's. At first she was wary, reminding herself to be on her guard. But he was so genuinely enthusiastic that Mary was unprepared for his final *coup*. As though he suddenly regretted being carried away, Degas paused and then with lofty sarcasm said, "It has all of your qualities and all of your faults. It is the Baby Jesus with his English nurse." This left Mary speechless.

Once more she knew that, while it sometimes seemed that she couldn't live without Degas, she really couldn't live with him. When they were apart, he often wrote her the most delightful letters, not only about his work and hers, but filled with poetic and personal avowals of his love and deep devotion. She treasured these letters. But when they were together again, he could never resist for long the mocking jibe, the attempt to penetrate the armor of her pride.

Mary realized that they were both a good deal older now and that Degas would never change. She admitted sadly to herself that she could not change either. They were both proud and stubborn, quick-tempered and sensitive. Mary finally acknowledged to herself what she felt she must have known all along—that she would have to give up any idea of ever marrying Degas. It was best to keep on the way they always had, having good times together when they could, but being free to go their separate and independent ways when Degas could no longer resist his biting sarcasm and she could no longer take it.

That night Mary gathered up all her treasured letters from Degas and burned them in the fireplace. She was sad rather than angry. They were beautiful letters full of fascinating comments on art, but they were also so personal and intimate that she could not bear the idea of their falling some day into strangers' hands and being read by curious eyes. Besides, it would be sentimental of her to keep them to reread when she was old.

"If there's one thing I refuse to become," Mary thought, "it is a sentimental old lady."

CHAPTER XXI

Mary was accused by her enemies and even by her friends of being many things, but sentimental was not one of them. As the years went on she became more independent, frank to the point of being blunt, sometimes prejudiced, and often violent in her opinions. She grew more and more outspoken in her scorn of those she thought stupid or pretentious, but she was warm and generous toward her friends and others whom she admired.

She never gave a snap of her fingers for anyone just because he was rich or famous or was in the Social Register. Members of her family and some of her good friends had become prominent and wealthy and even famous, but she loved them for other reasons: because they were capable and bright, cultivated and stimulating, and because they were steadfast and loyal.

She was glad for their sake that her brothers were successful. When Aleck was made president of the Pennsylvania Railroad, she was pleased, not because he had the red carpet rolled out for him everywhere he went, but because ever since he had built a water wheel on their country place outside Philadelphia when he was young, she had hoped that his ability and drive and rare good sense would bring him a satisfying career. She was delighted that they shared a fondness for horses and she eagerly followed the fortunes of his famous race horse, Cadet.

Gard had his ups and downs as a banker. When his financial success was finally assured, Mary was glad but knew that no amount of money could change him from the loving brother she had always known. The only thing that she deplored about Gard was his passion for boats and the water. She was the first to admit that it was her fault that she could not share his enthusiasm.

When both her brothers kept urging her to come home for a long visit, Mary finally braved the dreaded and inevitable siege of seasickness and went to visit them in Philadelphia in 1898.

A notice of her arrival duly appeared in the *Ledger*, blithely ignoring her reputation as a famous artist.

Mary Cassatt, sister of Mr. Cassatt, president of the Pennsylvania Railroad, returned from Europe yesterday. She has been studying painting in France and owns the smallest Pekingese dog in the world.

172

Collection of Mrs. Fletcher H. McDowell, courtesy of the owner.
Photograph courtesy of Shelburne Museum, Inc. Einars J. Mengis,
Staff Photographer

"*Mrs. Havemeyer and Electra*" (*Mary Cassatt*), 1895
Mary Cassatt's portrait of Mrs. Henry Havemeyer and her
daughter

Mary read this little social note with astonishment, indignant at first and then amused. "It's all true," she said, laughing. "I *have* been studying painting and I do own a small dog, several as a matter of fact, but they are toy griffons, not Pekingese." Then she shrugged her shoulders and quoted philosophically, "A prophet is not without honor save in his own country."

That year in America Mary visited other relatives, too, and did portraits of friends in Boston and Connecticut. In New York she stayed with her closest friends, the Havemeyers, before returning to France.

Only one other time years later did Mary venture to make the crossing to America. This time she became so ill that it took her weeks to recover, but by Christmas she was well enough to enjoy the family holiday.

One night when Gard and Jennie gave a dinner party in her honor, Mary listened spellbound to the tales of another guest, Percy Madeira, the African big-game hunter. She was so enchanted with his stories of adventure that she refused to budge when the other ladies left the table to go into the drawing room for coffee. Instead, she stayed with the gentlemen, listening avidly while they had their brandy and cigars. It did not occur to her that the others might think her eccentric, and she would not care if they did. She was quite frank in preferring the company of interesting men to that of chattering women.

Mary found both of the Havemeyers congenial and stimulating company and was glad to go on art treasure hunts with them, not only in France but in other European countries as well. Louie no longer had to go without bonnets or

175

petits fours as she did when she was a girl in order to buy art, but she still put great paintings first on her list of necessary purchases and she still looked to Mary Cassatt for guidance.

More important, she saw to it that her husband was completely won over to Mary's quick mind, her taste, and her judgment; so that he, too, looked to her for guidance. In the world of business, Henry Havemeyer was looked upon as a cold, sometimes ruthless man. Mary knew him as a sensitive, generous friend, interested in music and learning by leaps and bounds about art. His wife knew him as an adoring husband who tried to give her anything she wished for.

Together the three of them, sometimes with Louisine's sister, Mrs. Peters, made many an adventuresome trip. In 1901 they all met in Italy and set out in search of treasure. They had agreed to travel light and avoid the luxury hotels. All of them, used to the utmost in comfort, were now willing to put up with all kinds of discomfort for the sake of finding the rare, the old, and the beautiful in art at the end of a journey.

They rode a primitive train to Venice that was more like a wheelbarrow than a train. They braved rainstorms, freezing weather, and skimpy cold meals consisting only of bologna sandwiches. There were false clues and disappointing excursions to remote houses where, it was rumored, masterpieces were for sale.

Once from Florence the eager group were taken out to a palazzo where they were ushered into a dark room and were disappointed to find only second-rate pictures. But

Mary Cassatt, searching in the jumble of mediocre paintings, exclaimed over a portrait that she was sure must be by a master. The *signora* claimed it was a Veronese, a portrait of the artist's wife. Mary tried to persuade the Havemeyers to buy it, but they did not think the artist's portly wife a beauty.

After lying awake most of that night, unable to forget the magnificence of the painting, Mary renewed her urgent pleas next morning at breakfast. She vowed that if the Havemeyers did not want it, she herself, even though she could not afford it, would buy it. She would sell something she already owned and cherished in order to acquire this Veronese. It must not escape them. Mr. Havemeyer, who had learned to trust Mary's judgment, capitulated and began negotiations for the portrait, which eventually became theirs.

Mary also converted both Havemeyers to El Greco and Goya, and tracked down some magnificent, privately owned masterpieces for them to buy. In Madrid she discovered a marvelous El Greco portrait of a cardinal in red robes. When she said that he was wearing huge tortoiseshell-rimmed spectacles, Mr. Havemeyer would not even go to see the portrait, though he did buy Greco's "View of Toledo" and a Goya painting of women on a balcony.

Mary could not forget the cardinal. She told the Havemeyers eloquently that the great artist had known how to paint the eyeglasses so that one forgot them and saw only the piercing glance of the eyes. She said she was sure the Havemeyers would bitterly regret not buying such a treasure. Louisine wanted it, but her husband seemed unconvinced. Then at the last minute, before they had to leave Madrid, Mr. Havemeyer relented, saying to his wife and Mary, "Go buy your old cardinal with his specs."

Mary rejoiced that they were taking back this and other precious cargo to show it to New York in their magnificent home gallery and eventually to all of America through gifts to the Metropolitan Museum.

Louisine Havemeyer made a discovery in her turn. Years later she found a modern masterpiece in Mary's storage room. One day, as the two women were going through old canvases, among the things they brought out was the portrait of Mrs. Riddle which so long ago had been done as a thank-you present for the Japanese tea set.

Mrs. Havemeyer exclaimed over the marvelous painting. Why hadn't Mary ever exhibited it? Why was it in hiding? Then Mary told the story of how Mrs. Riddle and her daughter had not really liked it as a portrait. As she talked, she again felt the sting of disappointment over their reaction. "Degas liked it," she added, brightening.

"And so do I!" was the response. "It must not go back into that dark closet. It must go where everyone can see it!"

The result was that it was shown at Durand-Ruel's, where it was such a success that both the Luxembourg and the Petit-Palais in Paris wanted it. But Mary felt that it ought to go to America, and when the Metropolitan Museum of New York asked her for one of her paintings, she gave them this "Lady at the Tea Table."

CHAPTER XXII

In the decade or so before the First World War, Mary Cassatt's reputation began to blossom in America as it had in France. She was frequently exhibited in her own country and was even asked to serve as juror in painting competitions. True to her old independent principles, she politely but firmly declined all such invitations. She still would have nothing to do with juries whose votes might keep out a worthy newcomer.

When she was at last awarded money prizes such as the Lippincott Prize in 1904 from the annual Exhibition of the Pennsylvania Academy, and another from the Chicago Art Institute, Mary refused them and urged that they be given instead to young and struggling artists.

Of the two honors she did accept and cherish, one came from France and one from her own country.

In 1904, when Mary Cassatt was sixty, France made her a *chevalier de la Legion d'Honneur*. She knew that the red ribbon was rarely given to any woman, and for an American woman to win it was extraordinary. Mary could not help being pleased and proud. Carefully she put away the silver star enameled in white with its five double rays, crowned with oak and laurel. On special occasions she pinned to the left side of her gown the red moiré ribbon that identified a *chevalier*. She was pleased when her old friend Clemenceau said that he did not need to see her wearing the red ribbon to know that she was a great artist.

In 1914, toward the end of her career, Mary was given a Gold Medal of Honor by the institution that had seen the very beginning of that career—the Pennsylvania Academy of the Fine Arts. In this way the Academy recognized its former student not only as a fine contemporary artist of international reputation but also as one who had helped to bring some of the best European art to America. Mary was delighted to be able to reword in her mind the old quotation: "A prophet is *not* without honor *even* in his own country."

Mary Cassatt began to hear of another American woman living in Paris who was becoming something of a patroness of the arts. This was Gertrude Stein, a writer, who with her brother was collecting *avant-garde* art—early Picassos and Matisses, works of unknown artists. Mary was put off by what she heard about the unconventional Steins and their brown corduroy clothes and sandals, whose way of life was

"Young Mother and Two Children" *(Mary Cassatt), 1908*

"Child in a Straw Hat" (*Mary Cassatt*), *1886*

so at odds with the standards of behavior with which Mary had been raised and which she valued. It seemed to her they were interested only in sensational art.

The Steins held open house on Saturday evening, and Mary had some doubt as to whether people went more to see the strange paintings or to devour spreads of bread, ham, and cheese. In spite of her skepticism, she was persuaded by an American friend to meet Gertrude Stein, chiefly because Miss Stein seemed to be the only other American in Paris who had, like Mary, been born in Allegheny, Pennsylvania. As it turned out, their birthplace was the only thing these two independent women had in common.

The overheated apartment was crowded with Bohemian-looking people Mary had never seen before, speaking Russian, German, Polish—everything but French and English. Leo Stein sat in a chair with his feet up all evening. Gertrude reclined heavily on a chaise longue, talking in her cryptic way to those who came up to speak to her. When she and Mary met, they agreed on only one thing: that it was amusing to hear French officials attempt to pronounce the word "Allegheny," when they read it on the documents that as foreigners the Americans were always being asked to fill out. Gertrude's laugh boomed out like a foghorn.

Mary was elbowed about in the congested room, trying to look over people's shoulders at the paintings on the walls. The only one that appealed to her was a Cézanne portrait of his wife—but then she couldn't really study any of them in that milling mob.

Finally Mary begged her friend to take her home, saying, "I have never seen so many dreadful paintings in one place; I have never seen so many dreadful people gathered together.''

For days afterward Mary asked herself painful questions: Was the world changing completely? Was her kind of art going to be left behind? But surely, she thought, there would always be a place for the sunlit Impressionists, for the superb drawing of a Degas, even for the meticulous rendering of line and design that she had always tried for.

Poor Degas was rapidly going blind. Mary admired his spirit as he again took up sculpture, seeing with his fingers if not with his eyes as he made enchanting dancers in wax. The last time Mary saw him she was shocked at how fast he was failing. He wandered the streets of Paris like a lost soul, looking, someone said, like King Lear with white hair and beard blowing. He lost all interest in living and became obsessed by the idea of death, following funeral processions for people he had never known.

He no longer wanted to see his old friends, not even Mary. Because her own eyes were giving her more and more trouble, she longed to go see Degas to let him know that she understood what he was going through. But he cut himself off from everyone.

Personal troubles were suddenly submerged when once again black war clouds burst over France. This time Mary resolved not to run away. Whatever happened, she was determined to stick it out.

CHAPTER XXIII

Mary took refuge in her château in the country and did what she could to help the village families whose young men were all called up by the army. Her faithful companion and maid for many years, Mathilde, was deported to Italy and then Switzerland for the duration of the war because she was a native of Germany. Even when Mary's château became part of the army zone and she could hear the booming guns only fifty miles away, she resolved to stay in the huge, almost empty house. But the military finally made her leave and helped her to get down to Grasse, away from the fighting.

She knew that she could not take her collection of paintings with her, but neither could she bear to leave them behind. She had them quickly but carefully wrapped and

then, with her driver's help, hid them in the woodshed under and behind the woodpile, hoping they might be over-
looked if the house were seized and occupied—as it was.
The pictures were not discovered and they came through
the war unscathed. Only one of the frames was broken.
Few human beings survived with so little damage.

In 1917 Degas died, a broken man. Stricken by his death,
Mary wrote to a young painter friend, George Biddle, that
Degas had been her oldest friend in France and was surely
the last great artist of the nineteenth century. She felt
deeply that there was no one to replace him either as friend
or artist.

During the war, Mary's eyesight grew rapidly worse
and, since so many of the expert eye-doctors were at the
front, she could not get proper care. She suffered even
more over news of the fighting, the wounding and killing,
and the blinding of thousands of young men. In a small
villa, Angeletto, in Grasse she felt herself growing old,
waiting for the peace that seemed so far away.

Her young chambermaid read to her in a halting voice
newspaper accounts of the fighting along the front. Mary's
old friend Clemenceau, was now premier of France. His
soldiers, listening to his mocking voice in the trenches and
inspired by his stubborn courage, called him "the Tiger."

Mary tried hard to keep up her own courage, but she
could no longer see to paint. She could no longer see the
magnificent views outside her windows. The fragrance
from the nearby fields of lavender, the spicy scent of carnations, that used to console her, no longer came to her
from the now neglected fields. Bravely she tried to keep up

Mary Cassatt in her later years, photographed at Arles

a correspondence with a few friends and relatives, but her handwriting became more and more illegible; she had to have the letters she received in reply read to her.

When in November 1918 victory came it did not bring back sight to the ten thousand young men who had lost their eyes in the war. Feeling poignantly what it meant to be going blind, Mary gave all that she could for the care and relief of the afflicted. Operations on her own eyes came too late to be successful.

Mary and the faithful Mathilde were glad to get back to Paris and the château in the country, but in her last few years Mary was desperately lonely. Both her beloved brothers, Aleck and Gard, had died. Occasionally a devoted niece or nephew, now grown up, would come to pay her a short visit. Occasionally, too, young artists from America sought her out, but she suspected that most of them were following those whom she considered false gods. When someone asked Mary if she didn't feel left out of the new world of art, she gave vent to her feelings about that new world where, she said, no one knew how to draw like Degas, no one seemed willing to undergo rigorous training, and everyone was turning his back on the masterpieces which, after all, could not be surpassed as teachers.

All her life her work had come first with her—her work and her family. Now she could no longer see to work, she no longer had a family. Bitterly she thought how wrong she had been not to marry and have children. Wasn't that the only sure way to have a future?

In the country she had few visitors. A misunderstanding had estranged her from her old friend Louisine Havemeyer. A priest, the only intellectual in the village, came every Friday for lunch and for conversation. Still, Mary was hungry for good stimulating talk about art; she was starved for someone with whom she could have spirited arguments. Once when George Biddle, her young artist friend from Philadelphia, called on her, she couldn't stop talking. It was as though he let loose a torrent of talk that had been dammed up for a long time. Her eyes may have been blank, but her mind was as sharp as ever.

In the long intervals of solitude when Mary had no one to talk to about art, time passed slowly. She could not work, she could not read, she could not look at the prints and paintings that hung on her walls. She could not even see the splendid pastels by Degas that she had bought or that he had given her. But they were, after all, engraved on her mind. She remembered every superb line in every one of them and was consoled by what she saw with her mind's eye. She enjoyed, too, her dogs who gathered around her chair, flopping at her feet like shaggy shawls, warm and comforting.

In summer Mary took pleasure in her roses. She did not need her sight to tell the palest yellow from the deepest red or the most glowing pink. By their shape and their scent and her memory she knew each one. Long before, when her rose garden was first being planted, she said, "There is nothing like making pictures with real things." Her roses still made pictures for her.

In June 1926, Mary Cassatt died at the age of eighty-two at her château. She was buried in the cemetery near the village in the family vault on which are these words, reminding everyone of the Cassatts' American ties:

Sepulture de la Famille Cassatt
Native de Pennsylvanie
Etats-Unis de l'Amérique.

At the funeral services conducted by the Protestant pastor, many people came to honor her memory, including representatives of the Legion of Honor. All the villagers walked in the procession to pay their affectionate farewells to "notre mademoiselle" and to cover the grave with red roses from her garden.

L'Envoi

Once in a moment of loneliness and discouragement, Mary Cassatt cried out, ''After all, woman's vocation in life is to have children.'' In that moment of regret, she thought of herself as a failure because she had no children of her own.

Today her picture children are everywhere—in museums, in homes in France, in England, in many countries, but most of all in America where she wanted them to be.

Today Mary Cassatt's Château de Beaufresne is filled with real children, children who are very much alive. Like Mary Cassatt's small nieces and nephews of long ago, these children of today think the place a paradise.

When Mary Cassatt died, she left Château de Beaufresne to one of those nieces, Ellen Mary Cassatt Hare, the one who had grown to love the place in spite of falling into the

Courtesy of Musée Départemental de l'Oise, Beauvais,
and the administrators of Château de Beaufresne

Children at school in Mary Cassatt's former home, Beaufresne

pond and having to be fished out on her very first visit. As an adult, this niece took loving care of the château and in 1961 gave it to a charity organization that cares for homeless children, "Le Moulin Vert."

Now the château is home to fifty small boys who never before had a happy home. They live and study and work and play all over the place. They pick and eat the ripe red strawberries, they fish in the pond, they take care of the chickens and gather the eggs. They look after and play with the dogs, a goat named Bichette, and the gray cat, Monsieur Gris. They try not to bother the white fantail pigeons that strut about the courtyard.

Inside, they study their lessons—the first regular schooling they have ever had—and they draw and paint pictures which they put on the walls of their rooms. On fête days they pick roses as well as berries for the tables which they set up outside in the open shelter that they pretend is their American "ranch." For holiday entertainment they make up plays to present in their miniature theater, which they have proudly named "The Mary Cassatt."

These children look just like those rosy, cared-for, well-scrubbed children that Mary Cassatt used to paint—but to them she is not just a famous artist. They live in her home and they think of her as their godmother.

Mary Cassatt would like that.

BIBLIOGRAPHY

Baudelaire, Charles: *Art in Paris 1845–62,* ed. by Jonathan Mayne. Greenwich, Conn.: N. Y. Graphic Society, 1965.

Biddle, George: *An American Artist's Story.* Boston: Little, Brown, 1939.

Bizardel, Yvon: *American Painters in Paris.* N.Y.: Macmillan, 1960.

———: *Sous L'Occupation: Souvenirs d'un Conservateur de Musée 1940–1944.* Calmann-Lévy, 1964.

Boggs, Jean Sutherland: *Portraits by Degas.* Berkeley and Los Angeles, 1962.

Bottari, Stefano: *Correggio.* Milan: Edizioni per il Club del Libro, 1961.

Breeskin, Adelyn D.: *The Graphic Work of Mary Cassatt: A Catalogue Raisonné.* N.Y.: H. Bittner, 1948.

———: *Mary Cassatt: A Catalogue Raisonné of the Oils, Pastels, Watercolors, and Drawings.* Washington: Smithsonian Institution Press, 1970.

Breuning, Margaret: *Mary Cassatt.* N. Y.: Hyperion Press, 1944.

Brinnin, John Malcolm: *The Third Rose: Gertrude Stein and Her World.* Boston: Little, Brown, 1959.

Brinton, Selwyn: *Correggio.* London: George Newnes, n.d.

198

Browse, Lillian: *Degas Dancers*. N.Y.: Studio Publications, 194–

Burr, Anna Robeson: *Portrait of a Banker: James Stillman*. N.Y.: Duffield, 1927.

Carson, Julia M. H.: *Mary Cassatt*. N.Y.: David McKay, 1966.

Chase, Alice Elizabeth: *Famous Artists of the Past*. N. Y.: Platt & Munk, 1964.

Cromie, Robert: *The Great Chicago Fire*. N.Y.: McGraw-Hill, 1958.

[Degas, Edgar] *Degas Letters*, translated by Marguerite Kay, ed. by Marcel Guérin. Oxford, 1947.

Degas, Edgar: *Huits Sonnets d'Edgar Degas*. N.Y.: Wittenborn, n.d.

Duret, Theodore: *Manet and the French Impressionists*. Philadelphia: Lippincott, 1912.

Elsen, Albert E.: *Purposes of Art*. N.Y.: Holt, Rinehart & Winston, 1967.

Friedlander, Walter: *David to Delacroix*. Cambridge: Harvard, 1966.

Gimpel, René: *Diary of an Art Dealer*. N.Y.: Farrar, Straus & Giroux, 1966.

[Goncourt, Edmond and Jules de] *Pages from the Goncourt Journal*, ed. by Robert Baldick. Oxford, 1962.

Grosser, Maurice: *The Critic's Eye*. Indianapolis: Bobbs-Merrill, 1962.

Halévy, Daniel: *My Friend Degas*, translated and ed. by Mina Curtiss. Middletown, Conn., 1964.

Havemeyer, Louisine W.: *Sixteen to Sixty: Memoirs of a Collector*. Privately printed for the family of Mrs. H. O. Havemeyer and the Metropolitan Museum of Art, N.Y., 1961.

Henderson, Helen W.: *The Pennsylvania Academy of the Fine Arts*. Boston: L. C. Page, 1911.

Huisman, Philippe: *Morisot: Enchantment*, translated by Diana Imber. N.Y.: French and European Publications, 1963.

Hunter, Sam: *Modern French Painting 1855–1956*. N.Y.: Dell, 1956.

Huyghe, René: *Art Treasures of the Louvre*. N.Y.: Harry Abrams, 1951.

Janson, H. W., and Janson, Dora Jane: *The Story of Painting for Young People*. N.Y.: Harry Abrams, 1952.

Laffont, Robert, and editorial board: *Illustrated History of Paris and the Parisians*. N.Y.: Doubleday, 1958.

Leymarie, Jean: *L'Impressionisme*, Vol. 1. Paris: Skira, 1955.

Maurois, André: *A History of France*, translated by H. L. Binsse. London: Jonathan Cape, 1952.

Moore, George: *Confessions of a Young Man.* N.Y.: Modern Library, 1917.

————: *Reminiscences of the Impressionist Painters.* Dublin: Tower Press, 1906.

Mount, Charles Merrill: *Monet.* N.Y.: Simon & Schuster, 1966.

Murray, Peter and Linda: *A Dictionary of Art and Artists.* Baltimore: Penguin, 1967.

Nochlin, Linda: *Impressionism and Post-Impressionism 1874–1904: Sources and Documents.* N.J.: Prentice-Hall, 1966.

Paris de 1830 à 1870, Vol. II, ed. by Charles Simond. Paris: Librairie Plon, 1900.

Paris de 1870 à 1900, Vol. III, ed. by Charles Simond. Paris: Librairie Plon, 1900.

Pennell, E. R. and J.: *The Life of James McNeill Whistler.* Philadelphia: Lippincott, 1911.

Pevsner, Nicolaus: *Academies of Art, Past and Present.* N.Y.: Columbia, 1940.

Pissarro, Camille: *Letters to His Son Lucien,* ed. with the assistance of Pissarro by John Rewald. N.Y.: Pantheon, 1943.

Pool, Phoebe: *Degas.* London: Spring Books, 1963.

————: *Impressionism.* N.Y.: Praeger, 1967.

Renard, Marie: "Au Temps des Poseuses: Reminiscences of Mary Cassatt, Berthe Morisot, Edgar Degas, by a Favorite Model." Paris: *Verve,* Vol. I, #4.

Renoir, Jean: *Renoir: My Father.* Boston: Little, Brown, 1962.

Repplier, Agnes: *Philadelphia, the Place and the People.* N.Y.: Macmillan, 1898.

Rewald, John: *The History of Impressionism.* N.Y.: Museum of Modern Art, 1961.

Rich, Daniel Catton: *Degas,* in Library of Great Painters. N.Y.: Harry Abrams, 1951.

Rothenstein, Sir William: *Men and Memories.* N.Y.: Coward-McCann, 1931.

Rouart, Denis, ed.: *The Correspondence of Berthe Morisot.* N.Y.: E. Weyhe, 1959.

Saarinen, Aline B.: *The Proud Possessors.* N.Y.: Random House, 1958.

Segard, Achille: *Un peintre des enfants et des mères: Mary Cassatt.* Paris, 1913.

Slocombe, George: *Rebels of Art*. N.Y.: Arts and Decoration Book Society, 1939.

Smith, Logan Pearsall: *Unforgotten Years*. Boston: Little, Brown, 1939.

Stein, Gertrude: *Autobiography of Alice B. Toklas*. N.Y.: Random House, 1955.

Sutton, Denys: *Whistler*. Phaidon, 1966.

Sweet, Frederick A.: *Miss Mary Cassatt: Impressionist from Pennsylvania*. Norman, Okla.: University of Oklahoma Press, 1966.

Tatum, George B.: *Penn's Great Town*. University of Pennsylvania Press, 1961.

Valerio, Edith. *Mary Cassatt*. Paris: Crès & Cie, 1930.

Venturi, Lionello: in *Les Archives de l'Impressionisme. Letters from Mary Cassatt to Durand-Ruel*, Vol. II. Paris, 1939.

Vollard, Ambroise: *Degas*. N.Y.: Crown, 1937.

———: *Recollections of a Picture Dealer*. London: Constable, 1936.

Watson, Forbes: *Mary Cassatt*. N.Y.: Whitney Museum of American Art, 1932.

Wilenski, R. H.: *Modern French Painters*. London, 1944.

INDEX

203

"L'Absinthe" (Degas), 76
"Lady at the Tea Table," 178
Lafenestre, George, 98
"La Loge" (Cassatt), 94–7
"Le Bon Bock" (Manet), 47
"Le Déjeuner sur l'Herbe"
(Manet), 47
Legion d'Honneur, 180
Lepic, Vicomte, 129
Leroy, Louis, 60
Lippincott Prize, 179
"Little Girl in the Blue Arm-
chair" (Cassatt), 93
London, 68, 115–19
Louvre, 6, 10–11, 22, 25, 79
"Lydia in a Loge, Wearing a
Pearl Necklace" (Cassatt),
94–7

Madeira, Percy, 175
Madrid, 177–8
Mallarmé, Stéphane, 103
Manet, Berthe, *see* Morisot,
Berthe
Manet, Edouard, 21, 29, 30, 47,
82, 89, 147
Manet, Eugène, 129
Matisse, Henri, 180
Metropolitan Museum of Art,
178
Millet, Jean François, 88
Monet, Claude, 59–60, 65, 86, 88,
97–8, 129, 134, 147–8
Moore, George, 82
Morisot, Berthe, 25, 63, 88, 97,
107, 129–30, 133

"Olympia" (Manet), 21, 29, 47

Palais des Beaux Arts, 5, 6
Palmer, Mrs. Potter, 38, 148,
151–2
Palmer House, 38, 40
"Paris Seen from the Troca-
dero" (Morisot), 29
Parma, 41–2, 160
Peale, Charles Willson, 12
Pennsylvania Academy of the
Fine Arts, 9–14, 17–18, 65,
179–80
Petit, Georges, 134
Philadelphia, 3, 6, 12, 22, 33,
40, 172
Picasso, Pablo, 180
Pissaro, Camille, 63, 82, 88, 129,
134, 143–4
Pittsburgh, 37–8, 40
"Portrait of a Lady" (Cassatt),
137
Print-making, 99, 100, 114, 139–
40, 143

Raimondi, Carlo, 42
Renoir, Auguste, 63, 82, 89, 129,
134, 148
Riddle, Mary Dickinson, 118–20,
123, 126, 138, 178

Salon (annual exhibition), 20,
40, 42–4, 47–9, 51, 56, 59, 63–
4, 72, 74, 89, 108, 129
Sargent, John Singer, 68, 71
Scott, Annie, 118–20, 123, 126
Seurât, Georges, 129, 133–4
Seville, 42
Signac, Paul, 129

B
Cassatt
Wilson
American painter in Paris